SCHAUM'S OUTLINE OF

Theory and Problems of
ENGLISH GRAMMAR
Third Edition

EUGENE EHRLICH

Former Senior Lecturer
Department of English
and Comparative Literature
School of General Studies
Columbia University

Schaum's Outline Series

McGRAW-HILL

New York   San Francisco   Washington, D.C.   Auckland   Bogotá   Caracas
Lisbon   London   Madrid   Mexico City   Milan   Montreal   New Delhi
San Juan   Singapore   Sydney   Tokyo   Toronto

ABOUT THE AUTHOR

Eugene Ehrlich, author of many books on language, served as Senior Lecturer in the Department of English and Comparative Literature, School of General Studies, Columbia University.

Schaum's Outline of Theory and Problems of
ENGLISH GRAMMAR

10 11 12 CUS CUS 0

ISBN 978-0-0713-5985-6

Sponsoring Editor: Barbara Gilson
Production Supervisor: Modestine Cameron
Editing Supervisor: Patricia V. Amoroso

Library of Congress Cataloging-in-Publication Data

Ehrlich, Eugene H.
    Schaum's outline of English grammar / Eugene Ehrlich.—3rd ed.
      p. cm.—(Schaum's outline series)
    Includes index.
    ISBN 0-07-135985-0
    1. English language—Grammar—Outlines, syllabi, etc. I. Title. II. Series.

PE1112.E33 2000
428.2—dc21

00-023193

McGraw-Hill

A Division of The McGraw·Hill Companies

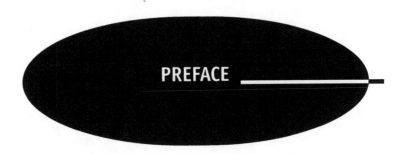

PREFACE

The study of English grammar has two principal advantages. It facilitates mastery of writing and enables students to study the grammar of other languages more effectively. This third edition of *English Grammar* was developed to make the study of English grammar as current and as effective as possible for all students, whether or not English is their first language. A Glossary of Grammatical Terms, at the start of the text, is provided as a reference to be used at any time. I hope that students will continue to find the exercises and explanations helpful.

Chapter 1 discusses the principal elements of the sentence, and the next six chapters provide information and practice in all the parts of speech: nouns and articles, verbs and verbals, pronouns, adjectives, adverbs, and prepositions and conjunctions. Each chapter of the book first presents necessary definitions and discussions, complete with examples. This presentation is then followed by exercises designed to help the student achieve mastery of the subject. Answers to all exercises are provided at the end of the book. The student is advised to work step by step through each chapter, doing each exercise in turn and checking the answers before proceeding further.

The previous editions of *Schaum's Outline of English Grammar* were originally written by Daniel Murphy and by me. Professor Murphy, my longtime colleague, now is deceased, so this new edition is dedicated to him.

EUGENE EHRLICH

CONTENTS

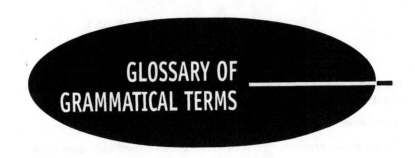

GLOSSARY OF GRAMMATICAL TERMS

Accusative case.   Form of a pronoun showing that the pronoun is the object of a verb or preposition: *me, her, him, us, them, whom*. Also called objective case.

Active voice. See **Voice.**

Adjective.   Word or words used to modify a noun, pronoun, or verbal: *good food, wonderful you, poor fishing*.

Adjective clause.   Subordinate clause used as adjective: Everyone *who approves* should vote for him.

Adjective phrase.   Phrase used as adjective: The woman *in the red dress* is beautiful.

Adverb.   Word or words used to modify a verb, verbal, adjective, adverb, or entire clause or sentence: run *quickly*, to sit *quietly*, *quite* fresh, *naturally* he was elated.

Adverbial clause.   Subordinate clause used as adverb: John left *whenever he felt like it.*

Adverbial phrase.   Phrase used as adverb: She sent her son *to the store.*

Antecedent.   Word or words to which a pronoun refers: *Alice* (antecedent) asked for *her* (pronoun).

Apposition.   Placement of a noun or noun substitute next to another to explain or identify it: New York, *the Empire State*; Richard *the Lion Hearted. The Empire State* and *the Lion Hearted* are known as appositives.

Article.   *A, an,* and *the* are articles. Their function is to modify a noun or noun substitute. *A* and *an* are the indefinite articles. *The* is the definite article.

Auxiliary verb.   Verb used with other verbs to form tense or voice: We *should* go to the movies. He *was* slaughtered.

Case.   Form of a noun or pronoun that shows function. The three cases are nominative (subjective), genitive (possessive), and accusative (objective). Nominative *I* saw. Genitive *my* hat. Accusative The dog bit *me*.

Clause.   Group of words containing a subject and verb. Clauses are either dependent: The man *who came to dinner* left early; or independent: *The milkman left two bottles of cream*. Dependent clauses are unable to function as sentences. Independent clauses are able to function as sentences.

Collective noun.   A noun that appears to be singular but refers to a group. Treated as singular when the group is thought of as a unit, treated as plural when the members of the group are considered individually.

Comparison.   Inflection of adverbs or adjectives to show degrees of quality or amount. Absolute: *good, quickly, famous*. Comparative: *better, quicker, more famous*. Superlative: *best, quickest, most famous*.

Complement.   Noun or adjective used to complete the meaning of a copulative verb. Also known as predicate complement: Fred is *sick* (predicate adjective). Norma is an *opera star* (predicate noun).

Complex sentence.   Sentence containing one independent clause and one or more dependent clauses.

Compound sentence.   Sentence containing two or more independent clauses.

Compound-complex sentence.   Sentence containing two or more independent clauses and one or more dependent clauses.

Conjunction.   Word or words used to join words, phrases, or clauses. Coordinating conjunction joins elements of equal value. Subordinating conjunction joins dependent clauses to independent clauses.

Conjunctive adverb.   Adverb used as conjunction. Most common examples are: *however, thus,* and *therefore.*

Coordinate.   Of equal grammatical or syntactical importance: two such nouns, phrases, clauses, etc.

Copulative verb.   Verb that links a subject and its complement. Most common copulative verb is *be*. Also known as linking verb.

Demonstrative adjective.   Adjective that indicates a particular noun or pronoun: *this* hat, *that* coat, *this* one.

Demonstrative pronoun.   Pronoun that specifies a particular referent: *this* is what I want; *that* is too much.

Dependent clause.   See **Subordinate clause.**

Descriptive adjective.   Adjective that names the condition or quality or noun it modifies: *green* trees, *wrecked* automobile.

Direct address.   Construction in which the writer addresses the reader directly: Dan, hand me the case. Ethel, please leave the room.

Direct object.   Word or words that receive the action of a verb: The speaker hit the *table*. He believed *that the boy would return the book.*

Gender.   Of no consequence in English grammar. Refers to masculine, feminine, neuter nouns in certain other languages. Personal pronouns in English have gender in third person singular: *he, she, it.*

Genitive case.   Form of a noun or pronoun used to show possession: *woman's, hour's, her, hers, his, their,* etc. Also known as possessive case.

Gerund.   *-ing* form of a verb used as noun or performing a noun function: *Swimming* is more fun than *lying* on the beach. They both love *boating* and *fishing.* Gerunds are classified as verbals.

Imperative mood.   Verb construction used in giving commands. The subject of the verb is usually lacking: *Go* home! *Stop* smoking!

Indefinite pronoun.   Pronoun that does not specify a particular referent: *any, anyone, each, everyone,* etc.

Independent clause.   Clause that can stand alone and convey meaning as a simple sentence: *She was fond of all her friends*, although she loved no one in particular. Also known as main clause or principal clause.

Indicative mood.   Form of verb used to make a statement or ask a question: She *drives* well. *Is* he still *baking* bread?

Indirect object.   Noun or pronoun representing the person or thing with reference to which the action of a verb is performed. They gave *me* a present. They gave a present to *me.*

Infinitive.   Simple form of the verb, usually preceded by *to*: (to) run, (to) jump, (to) attempt. Infinitives function as nouns, adjectives, and adverbs. Infinitives are classified as verbals.

Infinitive phrase.   Infinitive plus its modifiers and object: *to swim expertly*, *to read a book.* Infinitive phrases have the same functions as infinitives.

Inflection.   Change in form to indicate grammatical relationships. Inflection of nouns and pronouns is known as *declension.* Inflection of verbs is known as *conjugation.* Inflection of adjectives and adverbs is known as *comparison.*

Intensive pronoun.   Pronoun used to strengthen a noun or pronoun: the manager *herself*, you *yourselves*, the bee *itself.*

Interjection.   Ejaculatory word or expression: *Alas*, there's little left to eat. *Heavens above*, is there no shame in the man?

Interrogative adjective.   Adjective used in asking question: *whose* book? *which* street?

Interrogative pronoun.   Pronoun used in asking a question: *whose* was lost? *which* was stolen?

Intransitive verb.   Verb that does not take an object: I *smiled* all day. She *argues* well. All copulative verbs are intransitive. Many verbs function transitively as well as intransitively.

Irregular verb.   Verb that forms its past tense and past participle by a change of vowels: *be, was, were*; *run, ran, run*; *sing, sang, sung.* Also known as strong verb.

Linking verb.   See **Copulative verb.**

Modifier. Word or words that limit, describe, or make more precise the meaning of the words modified: *blue* hat, *the* man *whom you saw*, they walked *silently*.

Mood. Characteristic of a verb that shows the manner in which a statement is regarded by the writer. See **Indicative mood, Imperative mood,** and **Subjunctive mood.**

Nominative case. See **Subjective case.**

Nonrestrictive modifier. Modifier of a word or group of words already limited or restricted: Jane's father, *who rowed for Yale*, still rows every day. I brought him to my summer house, *which is in a Pittsburgh suburb*.

Noun. Name of a person, place, thing, quality, action, or idea. Nouns function as subjects, objects, objects of prepositions, objects of verbals, and adjectives.

Noun phrase. Phrase that functions as a noun: I enjoy *afternoon tea*. Will you be taking *the train to Denver?*

Number. Singular and plural aspects of nouns, pronouns, and verbs.

Numerical adjective. Adjective that numbers the word it modifies: *six* teachers, *first* anniversary.

Objective case. See **Accusative case.**

Parallel construction. Repetition of grammatical construction for coherence and emphasis: *flying* and *swimming*; *I came, I saw, I conquered.*

Participle. Adjective form of a verb. Present participle ends in *ing*: *running, walking.* Past participle ends in *ed* if the verb is regular, changes a vowel if the verb is irregular: *walked, talked*; *run, eaten.* Participles are classified as verbals.

Passive voice. See **Voice.**

Person. Forms of verbs and pronouns to indicate person speaking: *I am, we are* first person; person spoken to: *you are* second person; person spoken of: *he is, they are* third person.

Personal pronoun. Pronoun used to indicate people: *I, you, he, she,* etc. I saw *her.*

Possessive adjective. Adjective used to indicate possession: *my, your, his, her, its,* etc. *Our* hats, *his* typewriter.

Possessive case. See **Genitive case.**

Predicate. In a clause or sentence, the verb with its modifiers, object, complement, or indirect object.

Predicate adjective. See **Complement.**

Predicate complement. See **Complement.**

Predicate noun. See **Complement.**

Preposition. A word or words that convey a meaning of position, direction, time, or other abstraction. Together with a noun or pronoun and its modifiers, the preposition forms a prepositional phrase, which serves as a modifier: *to the front, from the shore, with them.* In these prepositional phrases, *front, shore,* and *them* function as objects of prepositions.

Principal parts of a verb. The infinitive (steal), past tense (stole), and past participle (stolen).

Pronoun. A word that takes the place of a noun: *I, it, me, he, him, they, them,* etc. See **Antecedent.**

Proper adjective. Adjective formed from a proper noun: *Japanese* restaurant, *English* history.

Proper noun. Name of a specific person, place, or thing: *Elizabeth, Finland, Empire State Building, Radio City Music Hall.*

Reciprocal pronoun. *Each other* and *one another.* Used only as the object of a verb or preposition: They saw *each other* regularly. We spoke to *one another* yesterday.

Regular verb. Verb that forms its past tense and past participle by adding *ed*: *worked, worked; talked, talked.* Also known as a weak verb.

Relative adjective.   Limiting adjective introducing subordinate clause: The woman *whose* family looks after her is deeply depressed.

Relative pronoun.   Pronoun introducing subordinate clause: The man *who* hired you has been promoted. The book *that* you gave me is missing.

Restrictive modifier.   Modifier that limits or restricts a word or group of words: Henry *the Eighth*, the man *who worked for you.*

Sentence.   Group of words normally containing a subject and predicate, expressing an assertion, question, command, wish, or exclamation.

Strong verb.   See **Irregular verb**.

Subject.   Element in a sentence performing the action indicated by an active verb; element in a sentence receiving the action of a passive verb: *Jane* saw her sister. *She* was received in court. Infinitives may also take subjects: Mother asked *him* to return home: *him* is the subject of *to return.*

Subjective case.   Form of pronoun showing that the pronoun is the subject of a verb: *I, she, he, we, they, who.* Also called nominative case.

Subjunctive mood.   Form of verb used to express doubts, possibilities, desires, and conditions contrary to fact: I doubt that she *will* ever *become* chairperson. If he *were* here, this problem would vanish.

Subordinate clause.   Sentence element consisting of a subject and predicate and functioning as a noun, adjective, or adverb: *That he was fired* came as no surprise to me. The book you *sent me* never arrived. He wondered *when he would hear of his appointment.* A subordinate clause, also known as a dependent clause, cannot stand alone as a sentence.

Superlative.   Highest degree of comparison, used when comparing three or more units: my *best* effort, the *oldest* child in the family, the *smallest* error. See **Comparison**.

Tense.   Characteristic of verb forms that shows differences in time of action performed: *I run, I ran, I will run, I will have run,* etc.

Transitive verb.   Verb that takes an object: She *bought* the *car*. Jack and Jill *carried* the *water*. See **Intransitive verb**. See **Copulative verb**.

Verb.   Word or words used to express action or state of being of the subject: Anne *studied* hard. She *is* willing. They *are going* home. The family *will have received* the telegram by this time tomorrow.

Verbal.   Word derived from a verb, but functioning as a noun or modifier. See **Gerund**. See **Infinitive**. See **Participle**.

Voice.   Characteristic of verbs that differentiates between the subject as performer of the action of the verb (active voice) and the subject as receiver of the action of the verb (passive voice). Active voice: The lecturer *elaborated* her main points. Passive voice: The main points *were elaborated* by the lecturer.

Weak verb.   See **Regular verb**.

CHAPTER 1

Principal Elements of the Sentence

A sentence is a group of words that makes a statement and can be followed by a period, question mark, or exclamation point.

The principal elements of a sentence are the *verb*, *subject* of the verb, and *direct object* of the verb or *complement* of the verb. Many sentences have only a *verb* and a *subject*.

Other important sentence elements are the *indirect object* and *modifiers*.

VERB

A verb is the word or words that describe the action or state of being of the subject.

Rats eat cheese.   (The verb *eat* describes the action performed by the subject *rats*.)

Marty has felt well recently.   (The verb *has felt* describes the state of being of the subject *Marty*.)

The organ was often played during chapel.   (The verb *was played* describes the action of the subject *organ*.)

SUBJECT

A subject is the person or thing that performs the action indicated by the verb or that is in the state of being that is described by the verb.

Trees and shrubs line the boulevard.   (*Trees and shrubs* is the subject of the verb *line*, answering the question Who or what *line*? *Trees and shrubs line*.)

Rare photographs are expensive.   (*Photographs* is the subject of the verb *are*. Who or what *are* expensive? *Photographs are*. *Expensive* is the complement of *are*. Complements are discussed later.)

1

DIRECT OBJECT

A direct object is the word or words that receive the action indicated by the verb.

> **Automobiles are destroying cities.**   (What is the action? *Are destroying*. What receives the action? *Cities. Cities* is the direct object of the verb *are destroying*.)
>
> **The gardener fertilized the lawn and the trees.**   (What receives the action? The *lawn and the trees. Lawn and trees* is the object of *fertilized*.)
>
> **The bank was robbed.**   (There is no direct object. This sentence has only the subject *bank* and the verb *was robbed*.)

COMPLEMENT

A complement is the word or words that complete the meaning of verbs that express *feeling, appearing, being,* or *seeming*. Such verbs are classified as *copulative*, or *linking*, verbs, which are discussed fully on page 41. Copulative verbs do not take a direct object. They are completed by complements. Note that all forms of the verb *to be* are copulative except when used as auxiliary verbs (see pages 41 and 42).

> **He seems well.**   (The verb *seems* does not describe action, but does describe a state of being. *Seems* links the subject *he* with *well*, and *well* is the complement of *seems*. Note that it occupies the position in the sentence that an object would occupy. The sentence *He seems well* can best be understood by imagining that a physician is receiving a report on a patient's health. No action is being reported, only a state of being. The verb *seems* conveys no meaning without a complement. Thus, *well* completes the meaning of *seems* and is called the complement of the copulative verb *seems*.)
>
> **He will be a carpenter.**   (The verb *will be* links the subject *he* with *carpenter*, a noun. No action is being performed. *Carpenter* complements—completes—the copulative verb *will be*.)
>
> **Emma feels fine early in the morning.**   (The copulative verb *feels* links *Emma* with *fine*, the complement of *feels*.)

It should be noted that the verb *feel* does not always function as a copulative verb. In the sentence *She felt the table*, an action is being performed, the action of *feeling*. In this sentence, then, *table* is the direct object of *felt*.

To find the principal elements of a sentence:

(1) Find the verb or verbs by asking yourself: What is happening? What state of being is indicated?

(2) Find the subject or subjects by asking yourself: Who or what is performing the action described by the verb or verbs? Whose state of being is described by the verb or verbs?

(3) Find the direct object of the verb or verbs by asking yourself: Who or what is receiving the action of the verb or verbs?

(4) Find the complement of a copulative verb by asking yourself: What element of the sentence completes the verb?

Note that a verb that takes a direct object cannot take a complement. A verb that takes a complement cannot take a direct object.

1. This exercise tests your ability to identify *subjects*, *verbs*, *direct objects*, and *complements*. You may want to review the material presented earlier before beginning work on this exercise. (The sentences include certain elements not yet discussed. They will be discussed shortly.)

In the following sentences, identify the principal sentence elements as shown in these examples:

Many cats have fleas.

Verb ___have_____

Subject ___cats_____

Direct object ___fleas_____

Complement ___none_____

Bill and Tom appeared happy.

Verb ___appeared_____

Subject ___Bill, Tom_____

Direct object ___none_____

Complement ___happy_____

1. Playwrights and authors receive acclaim.

Verb _____

Subject _____

Direct object _____

Complement _____

2. Libraries preserve the wisdom of civilization.

Verb _____

Subject _____

Direct object _____

Complement _____

3. Stores are busiest at Christmastime.

Verb _____

Subject _____

Direct object _____

Complement _____

4. Buenos Aires has the largest opera house in the world.

Verb _____

Subject _____

Direct object _____

Complement _____

5. Religion is a popular course in many colleges.

    Verb   _____

    Subject   _____

    Direct object   _____

    Complement   _____

6. Eli and Samuel were Old Testament prophets.

    Verb   _____

    Subject   _____

    Direct object   _____

    Complement   _____

7. Wars have produced death and destruction.

    Verb   _____

    Subject   _____

    Direct object   _____

    Complement   _____

8. Tamara telephoned her brothers.

    Verb   _____

    Subject   _____

    Direct object   _____

    Complement   _____

9. The waiter served mineral water to his customers.

    Verb   _____

    Subject   _____

    Direct object   _____

    Complement   _____

10. The dormitory was ransacked.

    Verb   _____

    Subject   _____

    Direct object   _____

    Complement   _____

11. Burglars were ransacking the dormitory.

    Verb   _____

    Subject   _____

    Direct object   _____

    Complement   _____

12. Helen studied Italian in Switzerland.

    Verb _____

    Subject _____

    Direct object _____

    Complement _____

13. She felt the lining of her coat.

    Verb _____

    Subject _____

    Direct object _____

    Complement _____

14. He felt well again.

    Verb _____

    Subject _____

    Direct object _____

    Complement _____

15. The defendants called their lawyer.

    Verb _____

    Subject _____

    Direct object _____

    Complement _____

16. An orderly mind ensures success in business.

    Verb _____

    Subject _____

    Direct object _____

    Complement _____

17. Microchips have revolutionized the communications industry.

    Verb _____

    Subject _____

    Direct object _____

    Complement _____

18. A bibliography is a list of books and articles.

    Verb _____

    Subject _____

    Direct object _____

    Complement _____

19. Even teenagers carry cellular telephones today.

Verb _____

Subject _____

Direct object _____

Complement _____

20. Few professionals in England now wear bowler hats.

Verb _____

Subject _____

Direct object _____

Complement _____

21. The shirt and tie suited him well.

Verb _____

Subject _____

Direct object _____

Complement _____

22. Outstanding matadors are highly respected in Spain.

Verb _____

Subject _____

Direct object _____

Complement _____

23. Many homes now are air conditioned.

Verb _____

Subject _____

Direct object _____

Complement _____

24. Air conditioning cleans and cools buildings.

Verb _____

Subject _____

Direct object _____

Complement _____

25. Although Polish, Conrad wrote in English.

Verb _____

Subject _____

Direct object _____

Complement _____

INDIRECT OBJECT

An *indirect object* is a word or words that represent the person or thing with reference to which the action of a verb is performed. You will encounter indirect objects in two different ways:

(1)   When an indirect object *follows* the direct object, the indirect object will be preceded by *to*, *for*, or *of*.

(2)   When an indirect object *appears between* the verb and the direct object, the indirect object will appear without *to*, *for*, or *of*.

Indirect objects occur most often with such verbs as *ask*, *tell*, *send*, *give*, and *show*.

Consider the following sentences:

He gave the job to me.   (The direct object of *gave* is *job*. *Me* is the indirect object and is preceded by *to*.)

He gave me the job.   (The direct object of *gave* is *job*. *Me* is the indirect object. Notice that *to* is omitted, because the indirect object appears between the verb *gave* and the direct object *job*.)

The professor asked her a question.   (The direct object of *asked* is *question*. *Her* is the indirect object. Notice that *of* is omitted.)

The professor asked a question of her.   (*Her* is the indirect object and is preceded by *of*. The direct object is *question*.)

Television commentators give audiences the news.   (The direct object of the verb *give* is *news*. The indirect object is *audiences*.)

Television commentators give the news to audiences.   (The indirect object *audiences* is preceded by *to*.)

Many florists send their best customers orchids on New Year's Eve.   (The direct object of *send* is *orchids*. The indirect object is *customers*.)

Many florists send orchids to their best customers on New Year's Eve.   (The indirect object is *customers*, and *orchids* is the direct object.)

2.   In the following sentences, underline the *indirect objects* as shown in these examples:

The bride threw her bouquet to the <u>bridesmaids.</u>
Tony Blair delivered a major address to the <u>House of Commons</u> and <u>House of Lords.</u>
We paid <u>her</u> many compliments.

1.   Central American countries provide excellent facilities for vacationers.

2.   The auction house sent the carpet to the museum.

3.   Attorneys ask their clients searching questions.

4.   The storekeeper sent his best customer a Christmas gift.

5.   Rebecca wrote a poem for him.

6.   He gave the museum a rare vase.

7.   The dog handler showed the English setter to the judges.

8.   She left her stamp collection to Marie.

9.   She showed her roommates her paper.

10.   He gave his Chinese vase to the British Museum.

11.   We supplied him food and drink.

12. Librarians provide services for readers.

13. District attorneys may ask embarrassing questions of witnesses.

14. Cargo ships usually give reliable service to most clients.

15. Children may tell their parents outrageous stories.

MODIFIERS

All words in a sentence that are not verbs, subjects, direct objects, indirect objects, or complements are *modifiers*.

Typically, modifiers define, make more precise, identify, or describe a verb, subject, direct object, indirect object, complement, or other modifier.

Modifiers may be single words or groups of words.

Consider the following sentences:

She ran quickly.   (The verb *ran* is made more precise—is modified—by *quickly*.)

She ran as quickly as she could.   (The verb *ran* is made more precise—is modified—by *as quickly as she could*.)

The blue hat suited the woman best.   (The subject *hat* is described—is modified—by *blue*.)

The hat that she bought suited the woman.   (The subject *hat* is modified by *that she bought*.)

The thief stole my new mower.   (The direct object *mower* is modified by *my new*.)

A thief stole the computer that Andrew's wife had given him.   (The direct object *computer* is modified by *that Andrew's wife had given him*.)

Copyright lawyers forward their findings to waiting clients.   (The subject *lawyers* is modified by *Copyright*, and the indirect object *clients* is modified by *waiting*.)

Copyright lawyers reveal their findings to clients who pay their bills.   (The subject *lawyers* is modified by *Copyright*, and the indirect object *clients* is modified by *who pay their bills.*)

Sean appeared overly anxious.   (The complement *anxious* is modified by *overly*.)

My wife appeared anxious to an embarrassing extent.   (The complement *anxious* is modified by *to an embarrassing extent*.)

Excessively grateful people embarrass others.   (The modifier *grateful* is itself modified by *excessively*.)

Uninformed by any standard, he continued to pose as an expert. (The modifier *Uninformed* is modified by *by any standard*. The subject *he* is modified by *Uninformed by any standard*.)

3. In the following sentences, underline the *single-word modifiers* as shown in these examples:

Three <u>large</u> stores were opened <u>simultaneously</u>.

The <u>open</u> book lay on the <u>professor's</u> desk.

1. An outdoor market attracts enthusiastic visitors.

2. The patient child greeted her joyfully.

3. The tired wife came home very late.

4. A tasty spaghetti dinner is always welcome.

5. A regularly serviced car makes driving safer.

6. Susan opened the large package carefully.

7. The neighborhood store opened early and closed late.

8. Grandmother always folded clean sheets neatly.

9. I never believe news stories.

10. Our best skater almost fell.

11. The trustees will meet tonight.

12. Our weekly newspaper prints only local news.

13. Nighttime television shows old movies.

14. Peter never repaired the broken pipe.

15. White wine improves roast chicken.

16. Herman's band was playing good dance music.

17. Bertha's diary has a blue binding.

18. I never saw him before.

19. The tall policeman gently comforted the frightened child.

20. Please bring two sharp pencils.

21. The red paint dries slowly.

22. The stormy weather raised high waves.

23. Happy schoolchildren study hard.

24. Robert's old car needs new tires.

25. They sell a million bagels annually.

MULTIPLE-WORD MODIFIERS

Multiple-word modifiers are composed of phrases or clauses. A *phrase* is a logical grouping of words that *does not* contain a subject or verb. A *clause* is a logical grouping of words that *does* contain a subject and verb.

Consider the following sentences:

The house *with the gabled roof* belongs *to my cousin*.   (In this sentence, the phrase *with the gabled roof* modifies *house*; the phrase *to my cousin* modifies *belongs*. Notice that there is no subject or verb in either multiple-word modifier.)

The man *who just entered the room* went *to the hostess*.   (In this sentence, the clause *who just entered the room* modifies *man*; the phrase *to the hostess* modifies *went*. The first multiple-word modifier has both subject *who* and verb *entered*. For this reason, the modifier is a clause. *To the hostess* has neither subject nor verb, so it is a phrase.)

The girl *whose arm had to be set* awoke *in the hospital*.   (In this sentence, the clause *whose arm had to be set* modifies *girl*; the phrase *in the hospital* modifies *awoke*.)

4. In the following sentences, underline the *multiple-word modifiers* as shown in these examples:

    Grace clung to the arm of the boy in the football uniform.

    The expert who identified the forgeries was rewarded by the art collector.

    I find him guilty.   (none)

    1. The dress that the champion wore on the tennis court was trimmed with green piping.

    2. The man in the ski mask ran down the stairs.

3. He went out on cold nights without a coat.
4. The flanker of the visiting team ran around the right end.
5. The building in which we are living has been condemned.
6. A car that is double parked blocks traffic in the entire street.
7. The man carrying the brown portfolio left his papers on his desk.
8. Garbage had fallen across the sidewalk.
9. People of all ages enjoy swimming.
10. The cigar store on the corner sells newspapers from many cities.
11. A line of unemployed men and women waited at the office door.
12. The girl in the red dress walked down the street.
13. The light of morning shone through the window.
14. The rain we had yesterday left large puddles on streets all over the city.
15. The window box we planted is full of red flowers.
16. A pair of blackbirds nests under that bridge.
17. Students from our school always visit the museum.
18. The girl with brown eyes pointed across the room with her left hand.
19. The driver of our bus is pleasant to all his passengers.
20. Ida will have dinner at our house on Saturday.
21. A salesman who speaks only English cannot communicate with many customers.
22. The batter who hit to left field reached second base before the ball was thrown in.
23. A dog that is well trained obeys a well-trained master.
24. The priest in our parish helps everyone who comes to him.
25. A skier who knows what she is doing moves with great caution.

5. In the following sentences, identify *verbs*, *subjects*, *direct objects*, *complements*, *indirect objects*, and *modifiers* as shown in these examples:

The basement of the house across the street was flooded during the storm.

Verb	was flooded
Subject	basement
Direct object	none
Complement	none
Indirect object	none
Modifiers	of the house, across the street, during the storm

The quarterback passed the ball to the tight end.

Verb	passed
Subject	quarterback
Direct object	ball
Complement	none
Indirect object	tight end
Modifiers	none

The general was an able man.

Verb	was
Subject	general
Direct object	none
Complement	man
Indirect object	none
Modifiers	able

1. Lisa hastily wrote an angry letter to her mother.

Verb _____

Subject _____

Direct object _____

Complement _____

Indirect object _____

Modifiers _____

2. Beethoven is the greatest composer of all time.

Verb _____

Subject _____

Direct object _____

Complement _____

Indirect object _____

Modifiers _____

3. While I was waiting for Jon, I met another old friend.

Verb _____

Subject _____

Direct object _____

Complement _____

Indirect object _____

Modifiers _____

4. Michelle is the worst student in the junior class.

Verb _____

Subject _____

Direct object _____

Complement _____

Indirect object _____

Modifiers _____

5. The Democratic candidate gave an important speech on the radio.

Verb _____

Subject _____

Direct object _____

Complement _____

Indirect object _____

Modifiers _____

6. Nola gave Marla a very expensive present.

Verb _____

Subject _____

Direct object _____

Complement _____

Indirect object _____

Modifiers _____

7. The young woman rose from her chair near the window.

Verb _____

Subject _____

Direct object _____

Complement _____

Indirect object _____

Modifiers _____

8. Literary critics often are frustrated authors.

Verb _____

Subject _____

Direct object _____

Complement _____

Indirect object _____

Modifiers _____

9. A competent ornithologist identified many rare birds.

Verb _____

Subject _____

Direct object _____

Complement _____

Indirect object _____

Modifiers _____

10.   Emma Dally has written three interesting novels on modern English life.

      Verb _____

      Subject _____

      Direct object _____

      Complement _____

      Indirect object _____

      Modifiers _____

11.   Working far into the night gives Gary bad headaches.

      Verb _____

      Subject _____

      Direct object _____

      Complement _____

      Indirect object _____

      Modifiers _____

12.   Most Third World nations experience economic difficulties.

      Verb _____

      Subject _____

      Direct object _____

      Complement _____

      Indirect object _____

      Modifiers _____

13.   Old automobiles are a burden to their users.

      Verb _____

      Subject _____

      Direct object _____

      Complement _____

      Indirect object _____

      Modifiers _____

14.   Life has never been better for this generation.

      Verb _____

      Subject _____

      Direct object _____

      Complement _____

      Indirect object _____

      Modifiers _____

15. I always study at night.

Verb _____

Subject _____

Direct object _____

Complement _____

Indirect object _____

Modifiers _____

16. The new puppies are the envy of the neighbors.

Verb _____

Subject _____

Direct object _____

Complement _____

Indirect object _____

Modifiers _____

17. H. L. Mencken was an irreverent critic.

Verb _____

Subject _____

Direct object _____

Complement _____

Indirect object _____

Modifiers _____

18. Kate made attractive dresses for herself and her friends.

Verb _____

Subject _____

Direct object _____

Complement _____

Indirect object _____

Modifiers _____

19. Actors receive many letters every day.

Verb _____

Subject _____

Direct object _____

Complement _____

Indirect object _____

Modifiers _____

20. Poverty damages the lives of many rural children.

Verb _____

Subject _____

Direct object _____

Complement _____

Indirect object _____

Modifiers _____

21. We still go to the theater as often as possible.

Verb _____

Subject _____

Direct object _____

Complement _____

Indirect object _____

Modifiers _____

22. Commodity prices are high everywhere.

Verb _____

Subject _____

Direct object _____

Complement _____

Indirect object _____

Modifiers _____

23. When Dick cuts himself, he bleeds for a long time.

Verb _____

Subject _____

Direct object _____

Complement _____

Indirect object _____

Modifiers _____

24. Paper airplanes rarely fly for more than a few minutes.

Verb _____

Subject _____

Direct object _____

Complement _____

Indirect object _____

Modifiers _____

25. Fishing is great fun once you have learned the fundamental skills.

Verb   _____

Subject   _____

Direct object _____

Complement   _____

Indirect object _____

Modifiers   _____

CLAUSES

Like a sentence, a clause contains a *subject* and *verb*. It may also contain an object or complement, an indirect object, and modifiers.

A clause that makes a complete statement and can stand alone as a sentence is called an *independent clause*. A clause that cannot stand alone as a sentence is called a *subordinate*, or *dependent, clause*.

A sentence may consist of one or more independent clauses plus one or more subordinate clauses.

Consider the following sentences:

After she sat down, she removed her shoes.   (This sentence consists of a subordinate clause *After she sat down* and an independent clause *she removed her shoes*. You know from the previous discussion of *modifiers* that, in this sentence, the subordinate clause modifies the verb *removed* in the main clause. Note that both clauses have their own subjects and verbs: *she sat, she removed*. Note further that the independent clause can stand as a sentence: *she removed her shoes*. The subordinate clause cannot stand as a sentence: *After she sat down*. The subordinate clause does not make a complete statement but depends on the independent clause for its meaning. The word *After* connects the subordinate clause to the independent clause. *After* here is classified as a *subordinating conjunction*. Conjunctions are discussed in Chapter 7.)

We went to the movies, and they stayed home.   (This sentence consists of two independent clauses. Each clause has its own subject and verb: *We went, they stayed*. Either clause can stand as a complete sentence. Each makes a statement that does not depend on the other. The conjunction here is *and*, which is classified as a *coordinating conjunction*. Other coordinating conjunctions are *but, for, so, or, nor*, and *yet*.)

6. In the following sentences, underline the *independent clauses* as shown in these examples:

<u>We stayed on the dock</u> long after the ship had gone.

Even though I was sick, <u>I attended class regularly.</u>

1. Some of us liked the program that night, and many people were enthusiastic about it.

2. Many voters misinterpreted the remarks of the candidate, so she tried to restate her position.

3. While we walked home, we considered the problem carefully.

4. Willie lived a long and happy life, but his time had come to die.

5. During the years they spent raising their children, they had many happy experiences.
6. Cigarettes have long been known to be dangerous to health, yet many people continue to smoke.
7. He wanted to join her in the new business, but he had little capital to invest.
8. Although there was enough food to go around, its quality was poor.
9. His first remarks were greeted with derision, but the audience soon began to applaud.
10. Well researched papers usually get higher marks than hastily prepared papers.

7. In the following sentences, underline the *dependent clauses* as shown in these examples:

Most of the seniors will be graduated <u>before they reach eighteen.</u>
At every opportunity he derides his associates.   (none)

1. Most of them have been driving carelessly even though they passed Driver Education.
2. Aspens and poplars grow rapidly but are not useful in building.
3. They left California after their children finished college.
4. Sally never eats meat, even though the rest of her family does.
5. We decided that she was not a friend of ours and he was.
6. My wife can barely manage to get to her job at school, where she teaches remedial reading.
7. The mayor told her constituents she would surely meet the town's financial needs.
8. Supersonic transport airplanes have little to recommend them, since they save the traveler little time and contribute heavily to air pollution.
9. I have reserved two excellent and high-priced seats for tonight's performance.
10. The movie held all of us spellbound except for Rory, who yawned steadily and audibly from the time the movie began.

PHRASES

A phrase is a group of two or more words that does not contain a subject and verb. Phrases have many forms and functions, which are discussed at length elsewhere in this book. It is useful here to learn to recognize phrases and to identify their functions as *modifiers*, *subjects*, *complements*, and *objects*.

Consider the following sentences:

They hid behind the building.   (The phrase *behind the building* modifies *hid*. Notice that no single word within the phrase conveys the meaning intended by the entire phrase, which functions as a logical grouping of words that conveys a single meaning. Notice also that the phrase has no subject or verb.)

The horse in front will win.   (The phrase *in front* modifies *horse*.)

Eating apples has been called a sure way to avoid doctors' bills.   (The phrase *Eating apples* functions as the subject of *has been called*. Notice that words such as *Eating* often function as subjects, objects, and modifiers. In these roles they are classified as *verbals*. In this sentence *Eating* is a *gerund*, one of the three types of verbals.)

Her hobby was flying airplanes.   (The phrase *flying airplanes* functions as the complement of *was*, a copulative verb. *Flying* is also a gerund.)

Eileen wanted to finish her work early.   (The phrase *to finish her work early* is the object of *wanted*. Notice that *to finish* is an *infinitive*, which is one of the three types of verbals.)

8.   In the following sentences, underline the *phrases* as shown in these examples:

The children were taken to the store.

Winning the peace is more important now than winning the war.

She decided to spear an octopus for dinner.

1. We swam across the winding river.
2. After her divorce, all mention of her name ceased.
3. They saw themselves pinned to the wall.
4. The glider soared skyward, soon to be released by the towing airplane.
5. They baited the trap in hope of snaring something for dinner.
6. A simple country doctor was all she ever wanted to be.
7. Books were his best friends; time his greatest enemy.
8. A cup of tea in late afternoon enabled them to survive until evening.
9. In the library the boy found peace and quiet.
10. The captain ordered us to pick up our gear and retreat to the nearest town as quickly as possible.

CHAPTER 2

Nouns and Articles

NOUNS

A noun is the name of a person, place, thing, quality, activity, concept, or condition.

Person

Abraham *Lincoln* is known throughout the world for his humanity.

Cervantes created one of the great comic novels.

Students of logic study *Socrates*.

The *actor* portraying *Tarzan* has a simple task.

Pelé, the Brazilian soccer *player*, scored more goals than any other *player* before him.

Place

Lima is the capital of *Peru*.

Dublin experienced a literary renaissance just after the turn of the century.

Travelers find *Scotland* one of the most beautiful places to visit.

Colombia is noted for marvelous coffee.

Afghanistan is no longer visited by most tourists.

Thing

A *beach* is unsurpassed for relaxation.

A man's *house* is his *castle*.

Dogs perform an important function for the blind.

The *committee* gathered around the conference *table*.

Russians enjoy *tea* served in a *glass*.

Quality

I admire her childlike *innocence*.

A thing of *beauty* is a *joy* forever.

The *House* of Representatives sometimes appears to be *available* to the highest bidder.

She discerned *deceitfulness* in his proposal.

The *shopkeeper* accused the salesman of *opportunism*.

Activity

> *Fishing* had become a major sport.
>
> He made his fortune in *manufacturing*.
>
> *Leisure* has become increasingly important for the middle class.
>
> The horse *show* listed six events, of which *jumping* was considered most important.
>
> *Writing* is an art too often neglected.
>
> One of the best books on *cooking* is now out of print.

Concept or Condition

> *Christianity* is one of the major world religions.
>
> The newspaper carried major articles on changes in *capitalism*.
>
> Football is often a game of *inches*.
>
> Allied Armies invaded Normandy in *1944*.
>
> *Monarchy* was the prevailing form of *government* in Europe at that *time*.

1. In the following sentences, underline all *nouns* as shown in these examples:

> <u>Intellect</u> alone never provides an adequate <u>answer.</u>
>
> <u>Actors</u> must study <u>voice</u> in <u>order</u> to be heard.

   1. Harpo Marx was a beloved comedian.
   2. The sky seemed to be full of parachutes.
   3. Take-out cuisine features hamburgers and chicken wings.
   4. Bill wore a tweed coat that once belonged to his father.
   5. Charity begins at home.
   6. The football bounced off the statue of Hamilton.
   7. The avenue is undergoing restoration.
   8. The boring speech lasted nearly one hour.
   9. Some chairmen fail to keep order.
   10. Our puppy has black spots on its nose.
   11. His hotel was near the casino.
   12. My neighbor drives a small car.
   13. Will the world ever forget Martin Luther King?
   14. Love makes the world go round.
   15. Ballpoint pens do not flatter the handwriting.
   16. The train may get us to Chicago in time to catch the show.
   17. Mary is allergic to roses, but she still loves them.
   18. The cleaning fluid did not take out the stain.
   19. A woman who misses her bus may well be in danger.
   20. Lois found that no one would offer her a seat.
   21. Mary refused to knit the sweater for her father.
   22. Joe changed the tire and got back into his car.
   23. He washed his hands as thoroughly as he could.

24. Bridge is not my cup of tea.
25. Planning seems to take all my time.

NOUN FUNCTIONS

A noun can have many functions in a sentence:

(1) subject of a verb,
(2) direct object of a verb,
(3) object of a preposition,
(4) object of a verbal (gerund, infinitive, participle),
(5) indirect object of a verb,
(6) predicate complement (complement of a copulative verb),
(7) modifier of another noun.

Subject of a Verb

Houses built after 1950 *are* usually of poor construction.   (Subject *Houses*, verb *are*.)
Beauty is in the eyes of the beholder.
Indian *art has* many admirers.
Despite all assurances, the young *dancer found* his debut trying.
New York City appears to have reached a stable size.
Swimming was his greatest pleasure.   (The gerund *Swimming* functions here as subject of *was*.)

Direct Object of a Verb

The hunter *shot* three *deer*.   (Verb *shot*, direct object *deer*.)
The automobile *forced* the *cows* off the road.
African hunters *found agriculture* impossible to sustain.
Critical acclaim too early in a career *may impede* a novelist's *development*.
Inadequate education *may cause delinquency*.
They *liked dancing*.   (The gerund *dancing* functions here as the direct object of *liked*.)

Object of a Preposition

They walked *about* the *mall*.   (Preposition *about*, object of preposition *mall*.)
For his *part*, he would remember that day forever.
Up and *down* the *river*, there was nothing but solid ice.
She performed most *of* her *chores during* the *afternoon*. (Preposition *of*, object of preposition *chores*; preposition *during*, object of preposition *afternoon*.)
The couple decided to ski the upper slope *before lunch*.

Object of a Verbal

Swimming the *channel* was more than he could manage.   (Verbal *Swimming*; *channel*, object of the verbal *swimming*.)
To pass his *examinations* easily was all he wanted.
Fighting the *rain*, he slowly made his way home.
Having found his *wallet*, he decided to retire for the night.
The consulting engineer offered yet another suggestion for *solving* the *problem*.

Indirect Object of a Verb

    The lawyer *gave* her *secretary* a brief letter. (Verb *gave*, indirect object *secretary*.)

    We *showed* the *curator* the new acquisition.

    The pitcher *threw* the *fielder* the ball.

    The messenger *gave Juan* an envelope.

    Teachers *assign* their *classes* enough work to keep anyone busy.

    In all these sentences, the word order can be rearranged so that the indirect object can be made the object of a preposition: The lawyer gave a brief letter *to her secretary*. We showed the new acquisition *to the curator*. The pitcher threw the ball *to the fielder*. The messenger gave an envelope *to Juan*. Teachers assign *to their classes* enough work to keep anyone busy.

Predicate Complement

    In the eyes of many of her clients, she *is* the best *lawyer* in town. (Verb *is*, predicate complement *lawyer*. The verb *is* is, of course, a copulative verb.)

    Christianity *is* the *religion* of many Europeans.

    She *is* the youngest *teacher* in our school.

    The main difficulty of that country *is* the *poverty* of most of the population.

    Word processors *can be* a *blessing* for those of us who write illegibly.

Modifier of Another Noun

    Stone walls were built throughout New England. (Noun *Stone*, modifying noun *walls*.)

    ·The *peace* talks settled the long war.

    Glass doors were installed in the kitchen.

    Tennis champions played many tournaments that year.

    John collected *postage* stamps.

2. In the following sentences, underline *nouns* and identify their *functions* in respective order as shown in these examples:

Utamaro was one of the greatest artists of Japan.

        subject of verb: Utamaro

        object of preposition: artists

        object of preposition: Japan

The college has graduated many noted scholars.

        subject of verb: college

        direct object: scholars

Rosa sent her bloodhound to the veterinarian.

subject of verb: Rosa

direct object: bloodhound

object of preposition (indirect

object): veterinarian

To obtain a new halfback, the manager offered his star rookie.

object of verbal: halfback

subject of verb: manager

modifier: star

direct object: rookie

Jane gives all her admirers a brief talk.

subject of verb: Jane

indirect object: admirers

direct object: talk

Sven is an excellent carpenter.

subject of verb: Sven

predicate complement: carpenter

1. Librarians like to help serious people find books.

2. McDonald had a flourishing farm.

    _____

    _____

    _____

    _____

    _____

    _____

3. We went to the zoo on the first Monday of the year.

    _____

    _____

    _____

    _____

    _____

    _____

4. Piano music goes well with a glass of wine and candlelight.

    _____

    _____

    _____

    _____

    _____

    _____

5. All he said was that he thought we made beautiful music.

    _____

    _____

    _____

    _____

    _____

    _____

6. The child ran in front of the car before we had a chance to stop.

    _____

    _____

    _____

    _____

    _____

7. Father was annoyed because we stayed up so late to watch videos.

_____

_____

_____

_____

_____

_____

8. Louis tried hard to become a painter, but only succeeded in becoming an illustrator.

_____

_____

_____

_____

_____

_____

9. We rode up the mountain on a chairlift.

_____

_____

_____

_____

_____

_____

10. Attending church on Sundays was the custom in our family.

_____

_____

_____

_____

_____

_____

11. My wife likes to prepare elegant dishes.

_____

_____

_____

_____

_____

_____

12. He knew marrying Avis would change his life.

_____

_____

_____

_____

_____

_____

13. Please give Sam a ticket for the football game.

_____

_____

_____

_____

_____

_____

14. I will knit Alfred a sweater even though I really should knit one for my father.

_____

_____

_____

_____

_____

_____

15. In a large family, laundry day is an everyday event.

_____

_____

_____

_____

_____

16. Eyeglasses are not a sure sign of age; bifocals are.

_____

_____

_____

_____

_____

17. An Acura is not only a beautiful car, but a practical one if you can afford the initial investment.

_____
_____
_____
_____
_____
_____

18. Fine wine is increasingly made of California grapes.

_____
_____
_____
_____
_____
_____

19. Term papers really should be called research papers.

_____
_____
_____
_____
_____
_____

20. I fail to see the advantages of microwave ovens.

_____
_____
_____
_____
_____
_____

21. Sculpture is a useful and interesting hobby.

_____
_____
_____
_____
_____
_____

22. Despite the advice of his doctor, Fred went on smoking cigarettes until the day he died.

_____

_____

_____

_____

_____

_____

23. Cabbage is easy to grow if you have room for it in your garden.

_____

_____

_____

_____

_____

_____

24. Cindy had drunk too much bourbon whiskey.

_____

_____

_____

_____

_____

_____

25. The new couch fits right into our living room.

_____

_____

_____

_____

_____

_____

TYPES OF NOUNS

Nouns are classified as _proper nouns_ or _common nouns_.

A proper noun is the name of a _specific person_, _place_, or _thing_:

Michelangelo is universally admired.

She was a _Democrat_ in her youth.

Oh, to be in _England_!

Lincoln Center attracts many visitors to _New York City_.

A common noun is the name used for *any unspecified member* of a class of *persons*, *places*, *things*, *qualities*, or *concepts*:

> *Sculptors* and *painters* work hard for *recognition*.
> We all admire the *work* of fine *novelists*.
> The *city* was known for its ugly *architecture*.
> Oh, to be in a faraway *land*.
> Steep *mountains* challenge experienced *hikers*.
> The *museum* exhibited only some of its *treasures*.
> He flirted briefly with a *career* in *politics* in his *youth*.

Proper nouns are capitalized; common nouns are not, unless they are the first word in a sentence.

3. In the following sentences, underline all nouns and identify them as *proper* or *common* as shown in these examples:

Mary submitted her paper in a folder.

    proper: Mary
    common: paper
    common: folder

_____

_____

Thomas Edison slept only four hours a night throughout the major portion of his life.

    proper: Thomas Edison
    common: hours
    common: night
    common: portion
    common: life

1. The road was icy, so James advised his wife to have chains put on the family car.

    _____
    _____
    _____
    _____
    _____

2. Siberia supports thousands of migratory deer.

    _____
    _____
    _____
    _____
    _____

3. The Atlantic is polluted with congealed oil from New York to Portugal.

———————————
———————————
———————————
———————————
———————————

4. Many students cannot finish college because of the high cost of tuition.

———————————
———————————
———————————
———————————
———————————

5. Most physics textbooks, according to Lorimer, do not supply students with sufficient exercises.

———————————
———————————
———————————
———————————
———————————

6. Theater seats in England are so inexpensive that some tourists see a play every night of the week.

———————————
———————————
———————————
———————————
———————————

7. Rich people ordinarily find that expensive restaurants are eager for their patronage.

———————————
———————————
———————————
———————————
———————————

8. Few lexicographers see themselves as guardians of their language.

———————————
———————————
———————————
———————————
———————————

9. Bernard Malamud was the author of many fine stories and books.

_____

_____

_____

_____

_____

10. Roger Casement was an Irish patriot, an English traitor.

_____

_____

_____

_____

_____

PLURAL FORMS OF NOUNS

Most nouns form their plurals by adding *s* to the singular: *time, times*; *girl, girls*; *home, homes*; *bear, bears*.

There are exceptions to this practice:

(1) Add *es* when a noun
ends in *s*: *kindness, kindnesses*; *lens, lenses*
ends in *z*: *fez, fezzes*; *quiz, quizzes* (note the doubling of *z*)
ends in *sh*: *hash, hashes*; *flash, flashes*
ends in *ch*: *lunch, lunches*; *bunch, bunches*
ends in *x*: *mix, mixes*; *box, boxes*

(2) When a noun ends in *y* preceded by a consonant, change the *y* to *i* and add *es*: *harmony, harmonies*; *baby, babies*; *burglary, burglaries*.

(3) For certain nouns taken directly from foreign languages, form the plural as it is formed in those languages: *alumnus, alumni*; *alumna, alumnae*; *erratum, errata*; *stimulus, stimuli*; *phenomenon, phenomena*. There is a tendency to drop this practice and use the letter *s* to form plurals of words taken directly from foreign languages. Thus, the plural of *memorandum* is now more often *memorandums* than *memoranda*. A current dictionary will be useful in deciding questions of pluralization.

(4) Certain nouns do not change in forming plurals: *deer, goods, headquarters, scissors, species*, etc.

(5) Certain nouns that have come down from Anglo-Saxon retain their Anglo-Saxon plurals: *foot, feet*; *tooth, teeth*; *woman, women*; *man, men*; *child, children*; *ox, oxen*; etc.

(6) Certain nouns ending in *o* form the plural by adding *s*: *radios, cameos, videos*. Others add *es*: *potatoes, tomatoes*. Still others allow both *s* and *es*. Check your dictionary.

4.   Give the plural forms of the words and phrases in the following list as shown in the examples. Consult a dictionary if necessary.

day	days
hoot	hoots
wilderness	wildernesses
sleigh	sleighs
acre	acres
seaman	seamen

1.	fox		26.	axis
2.	chief		27.	locus
3.	attorney		28.	sky
4.	potato		29.	echo
5.	spoonful		30.	preference
6.	valley		31.	loaf
7.	formula		32.	life
8.	genus		33.	matrix
9.	addendum		34.	actuary
10.	knife		35.	basis
11.	laboratory		36.	neurosis
12.	vocabulary		37.	privilege
13.	absence		38.	freshman
14.	cupful		39.	parenthesis
15.	babysitter		40.	attorney general
16.	crisis		41.	analysis
17.	diagnosis		42.	psychosis
18.	synopsis		43.	thesis
19.	athletics		44.	chassis
20.	library		45.	quantum
21.	Jones		46.	Smith
22.	quota		47.	symphony
23.	datum		48.	ax, axe
24.	booth		49.	secretary
25.	buzz		50.	levity

POSSESSIVE FORMS OF NOUNS

Two rules are helpful in forming possessive nouns:

(1)   With singular nouns and with plural nouns that do not end in *s*, add *'s* to form the possessive: *boy, boy's*; *child, child's*; *Jane, Jane's*; *children, children's*; *brethren, brethren's*; *sisters-in-law, sisters-in-law's*.

(2) With plural nouns and with singular nouns that end in *s*, add ' or *'s* to form the possessive: *boys, boys'*; *girls, girls'*; *Russians, Russians'*; *Charles, Charles', Charles's*; *Yeats, Yeats', Yeats's.*

5. In the following sentences, supply the missing *possessive forms* as shown in these examples:

The music of the Beatles did not appeal to everybody.

The ____Beatles'____ music did not appeal to everybody.

A delay of one day will not bother me.

One ____day's____ delay will not bother me.

1. The shirt John will wear needs ironing.
    _____ shirt needs ironing.

2. The performance of both teams in the first half was disappointing.
    The _____ performance in the first half was disappointing.

3. Most meetings of the United Nations begin on time.
    The United_____ meetings mostly begin on time.

4. He objected to the reunification of Korea.
    He objected to _____ reunification.

5. Who has not admired the batting of the 1998 Yankees?
    Who has not admired the _____ batting?

6. John Ruskin was known for more than art criticism.
    John _____ reputation extended beyond art criticism.

7. The child of my next-door neighbor had a party yesterday.
    My next-door _____ child had a party yesterday.

8. The ambitions of most men are never realized.
    Most _____ ambitions are never realized.

9. The best dishes of our cook are reserved for nights when company is expected.
    Our _____ best dishes are reserved for nights when company is expected.

10. The poetry of John Keats will never go out of style.
     John _____ poetry will never go out of style.

11. With a little luck, the scrambled eggs my wife makes will resemble the real thing.
     With a little luck, my _____ scrambled eggs will resemble the real thing.

12. At midnight on December 31, I shall be celebrating with my family.
     I shall be celebrating New _____ Eve with my family.

13. The shoes Mickey wore had seen better days.
     _____ shoes had seen better days.

14. Retirement for the Johnsons did not last long enough.
     The _____ retirement years were too few.

15. Mr. and Mrs. Jones said all they could at the meeting.
     Mr. and Mrs. _____ remarks bored everyone at the meeting.

COLLECTIVE NOUNS

A collective noun may represent a group or class considered as a unit. Such a collective noun is considered singular.

A collective noun may also represent a group or class of individuals considered as individuals. In this case, the collective noun is treated as plural.

The writer must decide how he or she intends a collective noun to be understood and must be consistent in treatment of the noun.

Some of the most common collective nouns are: *army, audience, band, committee, couple, flock, group, jury, majority,* and *team.* These nouns may be treated as singulars or plurals. When a collective noun is singular, its verb must be singular. When plural, its verb must be plural.

The following sentences show both uses:

Singular

> The army *is advancing* slowly.   (The entire *army* as a unit.)
>
> The band *has played* well.   (The entire *band* as a unit.)
>
> The jury *has reached* a verdict.   (The entire *jury* as a unit.)

Plural

> The audience *are leaving* their seats now.   (The members of the *audience* are thought of as individuals.)
>
> The committee *disagree* with the stand taken by the minority.   (The members of the *committee* are thought of as individuals. The *committee* has not taken a single stand as a unit.)
>
> The young couple *were* unhappy with the apartment they rented.   (Both husband and wife, as individuals, *were unhappy.*)

Certain collective nouns, for example, *athletics, contents,* and *politics,* appear to be plural because they end in *s.* Yet they are treated as singulars when they are intended as singulars and, of course, they are treated as plurals when they are thought of as plurals. Again, the writer must treat them consistently either as singulars or plurals:

Singular

> The contents of the valise *was* examined thoroughly by the guard.   (The writer treats *contents* as a unit.)
>
> Statistics *is* not my best subject.   (The writer is discussing a discipline called *statistics.*)

Plural

> The remaining contents of the valise *were* thrown about the room.   (The writer is thinking of the individual objects that make up the *contents* of the valise.)
>
> Statistics *are* said to mislead the unwary.   (The writer is thinking of individual computations that together constitute what we call *statistics.*)

6. In the following sentences, identify the *collective nouns* as *singular* or *plural* as shown in these examples:

> *Humankind* is coming to a decisive era in its history.   <u> singular </u>
>
> The *public* makes known its wishes slowly but forcefully.   <u> singular </u>
>
> The *remainder* are going to be left behind.   <u> plural </u>

  1. In many universities, *athletics* is funded from football receipts.   <u>   </u>
  2. He decided that he would have to cut the *herd* so its weakest members would not deprive the strongest of food.   <u>   </u>

3. The *class* agreed that their teacher should be encouraged to permit early adjournment. _____

4. He asked the *group* to take their time in reaching a decision. _____

5. A minister may find that his *congregation* speaks with a single voice in parish matters. _____

6. The *team* has decided to appoint a new captain. _____

7. The *opposition* are meeting quietly to develop an effective strategy. _____

8. We wonder whether the *remainder* is sufficient to pay her way for the rest of her life. _____

9. The *majority* must soon decide how to proceed. _____

10. His *offspring* are now going their separate ways. _____

NOUN CLAUSES

A noun clause has a subject and verb and functions as a noun. Noun clauses are usually introduced by *that, what, who, whoever, whatever, why, when, where, how,* or *which*.

As Subjects

> *That a politician can act that way after years in office* never occurred to me. (subject of *occurred*)
>
> *Why he acts the way he does* mystifies me. (subject of *mystifies*)

As Objects

> She insisted *that she would change her ways*. (object of *insisted*)
>
> She insisted *she would change her ways*. (object of *insisted*)

As Predicate Complements

> Life is *whatever you make it*. (complement of *is*)
>
> You now are *where I would love to be*. (complement of *are*)

As Objects of Prepositions

> He is taking action on all the problems of *which you complained*. (object of *of*)
>
> I purchased the book for *which you bid*. (object of *for*)

7. In the following sentences, underscore the *noun clauses* as shown in these examples:

> His position is that he was not to blame.
> How he can achieve his ambition bewilders me.

1. Whether we go tomorrow or stay depends on my wife's health.

2. Walter insisted that we pool our remaining capital.

3. His answers usually were whatever came into his head first.

4. He feels unhappy about what happened during his job inteview.

5. Dick cannot be held responsible for everything his children do.

6. This building lacks what modern architecture can usually supply.

7. The librarian told me that the book was on reserve.

8. When the picnic is held is no concern of yours.

9. Whatever you do will surely affect the remainder of your academic career.
10. Whoever attends the meeting will have a vote in the election.

ARTICLES

There are two types of articles: *definite* and *indefinite*. Articles are considered modifiers of nouns and pronouns.

Definite Article

The definite article is *the*. It is used to indicate a specific class of nouns or pronouns or a specific member of a class of nouns or pronouns:

The whale is still an endangered species.   (The *whale* as distinct from other species.)

He gave me *the* assignment I requested.   (He gave me a specific *assignment*.)

The teacher gave *the* class enough homework for *the* week.   (A specific *teacher*, a specific *class*, a specific *week*.)

George Bush is *the* president I remember best.

They are *the* ones who own *the* property.

Omission of the Definite Article

The definite article is omitted when the writer does not specify a particular amount or quantity of the noun.

Teachers assign homework.   (An indefinite number of *teachers* assign an indefinite *amount* of homework.)

Salt is an important commodity.   (The writer has not specified an *amount* of *salt*.)

The salt on our table is rarely used.   (In specifying a particular *amount* of *salt*, the writer uses the definite article.)

Indefinite Article

The indefinite articles are *a* and *an*. They are used as modifiers to indicate an *unspecified* class or member of a class of nouns:

Ms. Smith gave her father enough money for *a* week.   (The *week* is unspecified.)

A steak costs $25 in some restaurants.   (This means any unspecified *steak*.)

Carpenters may never again be paid $20 *an* hour in New York City.   (This means any unspecified *hour* regardless of when the work is performed.)

Choosing Between *a* and *an*

A is used before a word beginning with a consonant sound:

A stereo played all night.   (Consonant sound *s*.)

He used *a* hammer to nail the board.   (Consonant sound *h*.)

A one-hour lecture is more than I can take.   (*One* begins with the consonant sound *w*, as in *won*.)

He was *a* useful person.   (*Useful* begins with the consonant sound *y* as in *yet*.)

An is used before a word beginning with a vowel sound:

She was *an* able person.   (Vowel sound *a*.)

He talked for *an* hour.   (*Hour* begins with a vowel sound *ou*, as in *our*.)

8.   In the following sentences, insert *a*, *an*, or *the* where needed as shown in these examples:

She gave ____the____ correct amount to me, but I dropped all of it.

The conductor found ____a____ discarded wallet on the floor.

His first job paid less than $6 ____an____ hour.

Ellen intended to do ____the____ best she could.

Acid rock is not ____the____ best music to play in __an, the__ emergency room.

Ballpoint pens have revolutionized _____ penmanship.   (article unnecessary)

1. My brother asked her whether she could spare _____ few dollars.
2. No one knows _____ trouble I have made.
3. The defendant decided to plead guilty to _____ charge.
4. Poverty does not always lead to _____ unrest.
5. One cannot live on ten dollars _____ day in Europe anymore.
6. The lawyer showed that _____ shooting was accidental.
7. _____ hour in her company goes by in no time at all.
8. Frederick considered it _____ honor to receive _____ Alumni Award for Service.
9. One of _____ cabdrivers warned me not to stay at _____ Gideon Hotel.
10. _____ ambitious young man should not work so hard that he damages his health.
11. Writing a letter to _____ editor is not easy for most of us.
12. One of my dreams is to have _____ seaworthy sailboat, _____ ability to operate it, and _____ time to enjoy it.
13. Many potential investors are frightened by _____ prospect of a major economic depression.
14. The doctor cured her of _____ tuberculosis.
15. Nowhere else in our town can one find _____ food as good as his wife's.

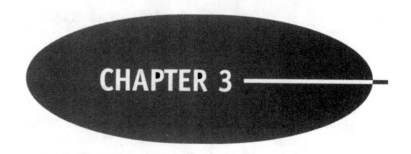

Verbs and Verbals

VERBS

A verb is the word or words that describe the action or state of being of the subject of a sentence or clause. The verb makes a statement about its subject.

Consider the following sentences:

Mrs. Carter loves her son. (The verb *loves* makes a statement about the subject of the sentence, *Mrs. Carter*.)

Politicians campaign actively for election. (Verb *campaign*, subject *Politicians*.)

Things are not just what they seem. (Main verb *are* makes a statement about its subject *Things*. The verb *seem* in the subordinate clause *what they seem* makes a statement about *what*, the subject of the subordinate clause.)

They feel well this morning. (Verb *feel*, subject *They*.)

The ship sailed last Wednesday for France. (Verb *sailed*, subject *ship*.)

All the artists have finished their paintings for the show. (Verb *have finished*, subject *All*.)

Each verb—*loves, campaign, are, seem, feel, sailed, have finished*—describes an action performed by the subject or describes the state of being of the subject.

1. In the following sentences, identify the *verbs* and their *subjects* as shown in these examples:

We dug for many hours and found nothing.

Verb   dug, found
_____
Subject   We
_____

Efforts in his behalf have proven fruitful

Verb   have proven
_____
Subject   Efforts
_____

Both gladiators remained on their feet for more than an hour.

Verb   remained
_____
Subject   gladiators
_____

The paint had been scraped from the building.

Verb   had been scraped

Subject   paint

1. Richard boarded the plane a minute before it left the gate.

   Verb

   Subject

2. Despite the attorney's eloquent arguments, the defendant inevitably found himself alone in his cell, unhappy and without hope.

   Verb

   Subject

3. The door closed silently behind her as she left the house.

   Verb

   Subject

4. As the bell in the tower tolled, the people gathered for prayer.

   Verb

   Subject

5. Eileen agreed that a trip to the college campus was worth her time.

   Verb

   Subject

6. The unsold books remained in the shop year after year.

   Verb

   Subject

7. Philosophy was his first love, but knowledge of accountancy earned bread and shelter for him.

   Verb

   Subject

8. Eat your breakfast now, or you will have no lunch money.

   Verb

   Subject

9. Our train never leaves on time.

   Verb

   Subject

10. The children played at their games until they were called home.

    Verb

    Subject

PREDICATE

A *predicate* is the verb in a clause or sentence plus all the modifiers and objects or complements of that verb.

A verb that has no modifiers, objects, or complements is referred to as a *simple predicate*. Two verbs that have the same subject are referred to as a *compound predicate*.

The sun *shone.*   (Simple predicate.)
The sun *shone brightly.*   (Predicate consisting of verb and its modifier.)
He *hit the ball.*   (Predicate consisting of verb and its object.)
He *is a great man.*   (Predicate consisting of copulative verb and its complement.)
Amanda *cooks* and *bakes bread* every day.   (Compound predicate.)

2.   In the following sentences, underline the complete predicate as shown in these examples:

Daniel has written many letters to us.
Veronique must leave for home.

1.   The lawn mower is no longer sharp enough to cut grass.
2.   City life has not improved her outlook.
3.   Fresh vegetables are hard to find in winter.
4.   I have not yet read the complete trial testimony.
5.   Professional sports has become big business all over the world.
6.   Can you imagine a world without war?
7.   Noisy dogs interrupted my sleep.
8.   Television appears to be the main interest of America's young.
9.   The farmer ran his tractor right into the haystack and ruined a week's work.
10.   Men's hats will one day reappear as a stylish fashion.

TRANSITIVE AND INTRANSITIVE VERBS

A *transitive verb* must have a direct object. An *intransitive verb* does not have a direct object. Some verbs function transitively and intransitively.

Consider the following sentences:

She ate the cereal.   (In this sentence, *ate* is transitive, since it has the direct object *cereal.*)
She ate for hours on end.   (In this sentence, *ate* is intransitive, since it has no direct object.)
The tree grew for many years even though concrete covered all its roots.   (*Grew* is intransitive, since it has no direct object. The second verb *covered* is transitive, since it has the direct object *roots.*)
Her gardener grew the finest tomatoes.   (Here *grew* is transitive, since it has the direct object *tomatoes.*)

3.   In the following sentences, underline the verbs and identify them as *transitive* or *intransitive* as shown in these examples:

Stray dogs often menace young city children.   transitive
Television and radio have helped him through lonely hours.   transitive
He sat alone all afternoon.   intransitive

1.   Cigarette smoke inevitably blackened his lungs.   _____

2. The automobile struck the wall head-on and burned. _____

_____

3. She smiled weakly at last. _____
4. Divorce hurts entire families. _____
5. The crowd indicated its approval. _____
6. The outgoing governor gave a memorable speech. _____
7. The stream ran through the valley. _____
8. Wars go on and on all over the world. _____
9. Their obstinacy incensed me. _____
10. The churches of Rome always attract many visitors. _____

COPULATIVE (LINKING) VERBS

A *copulative*, or *linking*, *verb* links a subject with its complement. The complement is either a *predicate noun* or *predicate adjective*. A copulative verb does not take an object.

The most common copulative verbs are *be, seem, appear, become, taste, feel, act, sound,* and *grow.* (Note that some of these copulative verbs may also be used transitively, for example, *taste* and *feel: This egg tastes good; I tasted the egg. The dog's coat feels smooth; she felt the dog's coat.*)

Consider the following sentences:

Now you are a man.   (The verb *are* is a copulative verb, doing nothing more than linking *you* with *man*, a predicate noun. The verb *be*, in all its forms, is copulative except when it is used as an auxiliary verb.)

She felt ill during the play.   (The verb *felt* is a copulative verb linking *she* with *ill*, a predicate adjective.) (See page 104.)

She felt the fabric.   (The verb *felt* is a transitive verb having *fabric* as its direct object.)

He acted morose.   (The verb *acted* is a copulative verb, with *morose* as predicate adjective.)

He acted the part well.   (The verb *acted* is transitive, having *part* as direct object.)

Thus, the manner in which certain verbs are used determines whether they are copulative.

4. In the following sentences, underline *copulative verbs* and identify their *complements* as shown in these examples:

They are culprits.
      culprits, predicate noun _____

A cup of coffee tastes bitter when it stands too long.
      bitter, predicate adjective _____

1. That tone sounds correct to me.

_____

2. Books seemed his only trustworthy companions.

_____

3. The dictionary became more important to him as he progressed in English.

_____

4. Some adults act childish when they are busy.

_____

5. The child's ability to grasp algebra appeared uncanny.

_____

6. Leonard was the only physician who was available at the time.

_____

7. She seemed eager to take the job.

_____

8. Anne's expression grew lively as she played the sonata.

_____

9. The dog acted sick after the veterinarian checked it over.

_____

10. Jon was the only middle-aged man in the room.

_____

AUXILIARY VERBS

Auxiliary verbs are used with other verbs to form the tenses, voices, and moods of those verbs. The most common auxiliary verbs are *be*, *do*, and *have*. Less common auxiliary verbs are *can*, *may*, *will*, *shall*, *must*, *ought*, *might*, *could*, *should*, and *would*.

Consider the following sentences:

I *may* go to the movies.   (The auxiliary verb *may* indicates a possibility of future action.)
I *shall* go to the movies.   (The auxiliary verb *shall* indicates an intention to undertake future action.)
I *will* go to the movies.   (The auxiliary verb *will* indicates firm intention to undertake a future action.)

Auxiliaries alter the meaning or time of the action of the verb: I *am going*, I *do go*, I *have gone*, I *ought to go*, I *might go*, I *could go*, I *should go*.

5. In the following sentences, underline the *auxiliary verbs* as shown in these examples:

He <u>does</u> want the car after all.
Hazel <u>can</u> have the job if she wants it.
Ed <u>is</u> studying French this summer.

1. Where shall we plant the rose bushes?
2. Can anyone in his right mind think that prices are coming down?
3. Where is she living now?
4. Learning to play the violin is more easily said than done.
5. Grammar is taught badly in most schools.
6. Many families have found their incomes falling in recent years.
7. Might I have a little more soup, please?
8. Do you exercise as much as you should?

9. Most teachers are made to teach large classes.
10. Would you accompany me to the movies?
11. She should find herself out of funds by now.
12. Corporate mergers have accelerated rapidly.
13. They will surely slave until they are rich.
14. The best of his fiction is ignored.
15. Music does not easily find its proper audience.

Shall and Will

Shall is used in the first person (*I, we*) in asking questions:

Shall I leave money for you?
Shall we depart now?

Will is used in the second and third persons (*you, he, she, it, they*) in asking questions:

Will you be able to find your way?
Will she have enough time to finish her thesis?
Will it be the only cat in the house?
Will they buy all the food needed for a week?

Shall is used in all persons for emphatic statements:

I shall do no such thing.
You shall not be permitted to return.
They shall not pass!

Shall is used in the first person to express future action or expectation:

I shall be seeing him tomorrow.
We shall probably meet you at the museum.

Will is used in the second and third persons to express future actions or expectations:

You will be with us this evening as usual, I expect.
They will certainly find their way easily.

Should and Would

Should is used to express an obligation or condition:

I should repair the hole I made in the fabric without charge.   (obligation)
You should pay more attention to all your studies.   (obligation)
They should clean the entire apartment thoroughly before moving.   (obligation)

If *we should* leave them penniless, they may actually starve.   (condition)

If *you should* disregard all their requests, they will no longer trust you.   (condition)

If *they should* find no merit in the application, his fellowship will be denied.   (condition)

Would is used to express a wish or customary action:

Would that *I* had spent more time with my mother.   (wish)

Would that *you* made decisions more carefully.   (wish)

Would that *he* were still with us now.   (wish)

We would walk together every day after I came home from work.   (customary action)

You would always remember to call on my birthday.   (customary action)

They *would* decline every invitation that did not include at least one meal.   (customary action)

6. In the following sentences, underline the correct form of the *verb* as shown in these examples:

If Jane (<u>should,</u> would) find her purse, she will never be careless about her possessions again.

All through those winters, they (should, <u>would</u>) prepare hearty breakfasts and ample dinners.

(<u>Shall,</u> Will) I ever hear from him again?

1. You (should, would) use your car sparingly if you expect to get through the year without getting deeper into debt.
2. When the horse (should, would) leave the starting gate, it (should, would) always head straight for the rail.
3. If he (should, would) forget his tickets, I give him little chance of making his flight.
4. Who (shall, will) enter the cathedral first, the bride or the groom?
5. Who (should, would) enter the cathedral first, the bride or the groom?
6. Joan and Sara (shall, will) compete equally for the prize.
7. Annette and Warren (shall, will) be on time or run the risk of losing their privileges.
8. (Should, Would) that she finally learns to keep her room in some semblance of order.
9. The youngest child in an ideal family (should, would) always be treated with respect.
10. The youngest child (should, would) always leave his possessions lying about, apparently in order to annoy his older brothers and sisters.
11. (Shall, Will) the club be able to reach a consensus on this matter?
12. (Shall, Will) both of us sell our apartments at the same time?
13. The faculty (shall, will) meet at its regular time.
14. I hope you (shall, will) join us for tea tomorrow afternoon.
15. They (should, would) share the bill, I suppose, since they indicated they expected to do so.

MOOD

Verbs make statements of fact and what is believed to be fact. They also express wishes, suppositions, doubts, commands, and conditions contrary to fact. *Mood* is the characteristic of a verb that tells the reader which of these functions a writer intends.

The three moods in English are *indicative*, *subjunctive*, and *imperative*. The *indicative* mood makes statements of fact or what is believed to be fact. The indicative also asks questions.

John Donne *was* born in London.   (There is ample evidence to support this statement, so the writer uses the indicative mood to state it as fact.)

Was John Donne born in London?   (This verb asks a question and so is in the indicative mood.)

She believes her physician *is* well qualified.   (Whether *she* is correct or not, the verb *is* indicates that *she believes* her statement to be true. The verb *believes* is in the indicative mood, because the writer of the sentence is reporting what she takes to be fact.)

Is her physician at her bedside?   (The verb *is* is in the indicative mood because it asks a question.)

The *subjunctive* mood appears in relatively few constructions. It is used most often to express conditions contrary to fact and to express wishes, suppositions, and doubts. (The uses of the subjunctive are discussed fully in the next section.) The subjunctive appears most often in formal writing and in the speech of educated persons. The indicative mood almost always replaces the subjective mood in informal writing and everyday speech.

! wish my father *were* still alive.   (This is a wish, so *were* is in the subjunctive mood.)

Suppose he *were* still alive, would he favor that action?   (The verb *were* is in the subjunctive mood because *suppose he were still alive* is a supposition.)

If this *be* treason, make the most of it!   (The speaker firmly believes he or she is not guilty of treason, but there may be doubt in the minds of others. The subjunctive *be* expresses this doubt.)

If Helen Wills Moody *were representing* us at Wimbledon today, victory would be ours. (The conjunction *If* introduces a conditional statement. Since Helen Wills Moody is not alive to represent us at Wimbledon, the condition is contrary to fact. The verb *were representing* indicates that this condition is contrary to fact.)

The subjunctive mood is distinguished from the indicative in the third person singular of all verbs and in certain forms of the verb *be*. The following table shows the typical verb *want* in the present tense and the verb *be* in the present and past tenses.

	Indicative	Subjunctive	Indicative		Subjunctive	
	Present Tense		Present	Past	Present	Past
I	want	want	am	was	be	were
you	want	want	are	were	be	were
he, she, it	wants	want	is	was	be	were
we	want	want	are	were	be	were
you	want	want	are	were	be	were
they	want	want	are	were	be	were

The *imperative* mood expresses a command or makes an urgent demand:

Leave the room!

Call an ambulance!

Let them die!

The imperative mood is used only in the second and third persons, singular and plural.

7. In the following sentences indicate the *mood* of each of the *italicized verbs* as shown in these examples:

> *Are* they really at home every evening?   indicative
>
> *Send* them to bed at once!   imperative
>
> I wish I *were* seventy years old again.   subjunctive

1.   They will remain together provided that Father *consents.*   _____
2.   If I *were* the boss here, I would do things differently.   _____
3.   Corporations *find* that the interest rates they must pay fluctuate widely.   _____
4.   *Are* you really *supporting* yourself comfortably by painting?   _____
5.   *Were* you the oldest person on the team?   _____
6   *Stay* away from television and cigarettes.   _____
7.   Some dictionaries *provide* guidance in correct usage.   _____
8.   As long as you remain alert, you *will find* the access road.   _____
9.   Wildflowers *give* us much pleasure.   _____
10.   He will be honored with a doctorate provided he *makes* a substantial donation.   _____
11.   Never *give up* the fight!   _____
12.   Swimming against the tide *fatigued* him greatly.   _____
13.   American history *has been* his specialty.   _____
14   If he *wants* to succeed, he must work.   _____
15.   If you want to succeed, *work* hard.   _____

Uses of the Subjunctive Mood

The subjunctive mood is used for (1) conditions contrary to fact; (2) wishes, recommendations, and demands in clauses introduced by *that* or in clauses in which *that is* implied; and (3) certain idiomatic expressions.

The subjunctive has few uses in modern English. More and more, the subjunctive mood is being replaced by the indicative mood or by simplified constructions that avoid verbs entirely. Nevertheless, good writing and speech still employ the subjunctive.

Conditions Contrary to Fact

A condition that cannot be true is known as a condition contrary to fact.

> *If I were* ten years younger, I would remarry.   (The presence of a condition is signaled by the conjunction *If.* Because the condition is contrary to fact, the subjunctive *were* is used.)
>
> *If President Lyndon B. Johnson were* still alive, he would find that many of the policies he followed are still in force today.   (Condition contrary to fact requires the subjunctive *were.*)

That *Clauses*

Clauses introduced by *that* or clauses in which *that* is implied frequently express wishes, recommendations, demands, orders, formal motions, or parliamentary resolutions. The subjunctive is used in these clauses. Consider the following sentences:

> I wish *that I were* prime minister.   (The subjunctive *were*, not indicative *was*.)
>
> I recommend *that he take* a trip abroad.   (Subjunctive *take*, not indicative *takes*.)

We demand *that they be silenced.*   (Subjunctive *be silenced*, not indicative *are silenced*.)

We ask only *that the most guilty be punished.*   (Subjunctive *be punished*, not indicative *are punished*.)

She moved *that parliamentary procedure be laid* aside.   (Subjunctive *be laid*, not indicative *is laid*.)

Resolved, *that a fifty-first state be admitted* to the union.   (Subjunctive *be admitted*, not indicative *is admitted*.)

The relative pronoun *that* can be omitted from the first three of the preceding sentences without changing meaning and without altering the requirement for employing the subjunctive mood:

I wish *I were* prime minister.

I recommend *he take* a trip abroad.

We demand *they be silenced.*

Idiomatic Expressions

The English language has certain constructions that remain fixed in the subjunctive mood. These idiomatic constructions include: *be* that as it may, *be* it said, *come* what may, God *bless* you, far *be* it from me, and *suffice* it to say.

8. In the following sentences, underline the correct form of the *verb* as shown in these examples:

I wish that he (was, <u>were</u>) not here.

I demand that she (<u>leave,</u> leaves).

If I (was, <u>were</u>) King, I would be the happiest man on earth.

1. Heaven (forbid, forbids) that she should marry a clone of her first husband.

2. I request that the Board of Elections (pay, pays) particular attention to votes cast in the Twelfth District, where all the town cemeteries are located.

3. I wish she (was, were) going to medical school in my place.

4. If she (insist, insists) on paying the bill, it will be all right with me.

5. If the theater (was, were) nearer my house, I would be able to walk there.

6. The judge ordered that widows and orphans (are, be) protected.

7. (Come, Comes) what may, I shall forever believe I mistreated him.

8. A member of the opposition moved that the meeting (be, is) adjourned.

9. We request that they (are, be) barred from the meeting.

10. I would make the situation clear to him if he (was, were) here.

11. I think James (was, were) sound asleep on the beach when the poor boy died.

12. I ask only that I (am, be) treated with respect.

13. We believe that the bill (was, were) counterfeit.

14. If he (was, were) here, he would make everything clear.

15. I recommend that he (apologize, apologizes) at once.

VOICE

Voice is the characteristic of a verb that tells the reader whether the subject of the verb is performing the action of the verb (*active voice*) or whether the subject of the verb is acted upon (*passive voice*). The passive voice is identified by some form of the verb *be* plus a *past participle*.

	Active Voice	**Passive Voice**
Present	he finds	he is found
Past	he found	he was found
Future	he will find	he will be found
Infinitive	to find, to have found	to be found, to have been found

(There are other tenses in English, of course, and they are discussed elsewhere.)

9. In the following sentences, indicate the *voice* of each of the *italicized verbs* as shown in these examples:

   They *have gone* home. ___active___

   He *has climbed* that mountain many times. ___active___

   That mountain *has been climbed* before. ___passive___

1. Politicians *are perceived* by the voters in various ways. _____
2. The voters *perceive* politicians in various ways. _____
3. Novels of quality *entrance* their readers. _____
4. When *will you paint* the exterior of your house? _____
5. Is your house *being painted*? _____
6. The barn door, of course, *must be rehung*. _____
7. Flies *carry* disease. _____
8. The meals *will be delivered* to the homeless when they are ready. _____
9. Many countries *are experiencing* severe drought. _____
10. Many countries *have experienced* drought. _____

NUMBER

Like nouns and pronouns, verbs have singular and plural forms. The number of the subject—a noun or pronoun—determines the number of the verb.

Consider the following sentences:

   I work hard.   (Since the subject *I* is singular, the verb *work* is singular.)

   We work hard.   (Since the subject *We* is plural, the verb *work* is plural.)

10. In the following sentences, underline each *verb*, and indicate its *number*, as shown in these examples:

   The cat <u>raised</u> its back high.   ___singular___

   The house <u>is</u> up for sale.   ___singular___

   Our neighbors <u>have left</u> for Florida.   ___plural___

1. They will be going home early tonight. _____
2. Nothing is better than blueberry pie and chocolate ice cream. _____
3. The Hudson is one of the most beautiful rivers in the United States. _____
4. Vermont and New Hampshire hardly ever cooperate. _____
5. Has your daughter been sitting there all alone? _____
6. Have you and Sue been sitting there together? _____
7. He will be leaving right after dinner. _____
8. They find themselves at a total loss for words. _____
9. Instead of a real lunch, we will be having pizza and beer. _____
10. This machine has seen better days. _____

Agreement of Subject and Verb

A singular subject must have a singular verb. A plural subject must have a plural verb. This rule for agreement in number of subject and its verb is easy to learn. Two sentences are sufficient to illustrate its proper application.

The skater has fallen through the ice.   (Singular subject *skater*, singular verb *has fallen*.)
The skaters have fallen through the ice.   (Plural subject *skaters*, plural verb *have fallen*.)

11. In the following sentences, supply the correct *form of the verb* as shown in these examples:

I (be) in complete agreement with everything you say.   ___am___
Today we (be) completely opposed to all your ideas.   ___are___

1. Cats (have) an extraordinary ability to get their own way. _____
2. A cat (have) complete freedom to roam in our neighborhood. _____
3. England (be) no longer a world power in the minds of many. _____
4. The countries of Europe finally (achieve) economic unity in the coming years.
    _____
5. Economic strength and political vitality (go) hand in hand. _____
6. Snow and ice (collect) in our driveway every winter. _____
7. Unpaid parking tickets (be) my greatest problem right now. _____
8. Ian (have) always been a good lawyer, the judge said. _____
9. Mark Twain still (find) a large readership among Russians. _____
10. Many countries of Africa (be) beginning to exploit valuable natural resources.
    _____

In many sentences containing a singular subject, plural words may intervene between subject and verb. In such cases, the writer must remember that the subject is singular and must have a singular verb.

Consider the following sentences:

The *importance* of men, ammunition, and food supplies *was* not *overlooked* by the general.   (Because the subject *importance* is singular, the verb *was overlooked* is singular.

The phrase *of men, ammunition, and food supplies* modifies *importance* and has nothing to do with the number of the subject and verb.)

The *safety* of her many children *was* her first concern.   (The subject *safety* is singular, so the verb *was* is singular.)

Another problem in agreement may occur when the subject of a verb follows the verb instead of preceding it.

Consider the following sentences:

There *were* three *men* behind her in the checkout line.   (The subject of *were* is *men*. Since *men* is plural, the plural verb *were* is used.)

There *was* little *applause* for the sopranos.   (The subject of *was* is *applause*. Since *applause* is singular, the singular verb *was* is used.)

Concerning the acrobats there *was* little *disagreement*.   (The subject *disagreement* is singular, so the singular verb *was* is used.)

Beyond the highway *stands* the ugly *slum*.   (The singular subject *slum* requires the singular verb *stands*.)

Across the plains *lie miles* of untracked wilderness.   (The plural subject *miles* requires the plural verb *lie*.)

12.   In the following sentences, supply the correct *form of the verb* as shown in these examples:

At the time of her death, Rose's principal hobby (be) all types of stitchery.   ____was____

On most subjects, Jane and John now (be) in agreement.   ____are____

He found that there (be) little use in continuing work on his novels and plays.   ____was____

The aggression he observed in apes, large cats, and other mammals (be) also reported by other investigators.   ____was____

1.   The first violinist, unlike other members of the string section, (be) not ready to play when the conductor raised his baton.   _____

2.   The first violinist and the entire string section (be) unwilling to rehearse, because the conductor is so difficult to work with.   _____

3.   Beyond the knoll (lie) deposits of rock of the right type for the beautiful house he wants to build.   _____

4.   The necessity of assuring adequate stores of food and drink (be) not recognized by many of the inexperienced hikers who undertook the climb.   _____

5.   Of primary importance (be) a supply of clear drinking water, if one is selecting a home site.   _____

6.   After the dinner, there (be) going to be two long speeches by the candidates.   _____

7.   Once the sap begins to flow next spring, there (be) going to be work for all of us.   _____

8.   After the principal address was given, there (be) few of us still awake in the room.   _____

9.   People are our main concern, even though there (be) many other problems facing us.   _____

10. Inflation and recession no longer (be) the most serious public concerns in our country.

_____

Compound Subjects and Their Verbs

A compound subject is two or more nouns, pronouns, or noun phrases acting together as the subject of a verb: *Jack and Bill, he and I, hearts and flowers, health or sickness, a pound of potatoes or onions*. Compound subjects connected by *and* usually take a plural verb. Compound subjects connected by *or* or *nor* usually take a singular verb.

When compound subjects are connected by *and*, they are usually intended as plurals. Sometimes, however, they are intended as singular constructions. The following sentences illustrate both types:

Plural

> Jack and Bill are going up the mountain.   (The subject of this sentence, *Jack and Bill*, can be replaced by *two boys* or *two men*, which would be plural. The compound subject *Jack and Bill*, therefore, is plural. For this reason, a plural verb is used: *are going*.)

Singular

> A hot dog and sauerkraut is all I want for lunch.   (The subject of this sentence is a single dish: *hot dog and sauerkraut*. The subject, therefore, is singular and the verb must be singular: *is*.)

When compound subjects are connected by *or*, they are singular unless the parts of the compound subject are themselves plural.

Consider the following sentences:

Singular

> A box of candy or a basket of fruit is always welcome.   (Both parts of the compound subject *box or basket* are singular, so a singular verb is needed: *is*.)

Plural

> Candies or fruits are equally acceptable.   (Both parts of the compound subject *candies or fruits* are plural, so a plural verb is needed: *are*.)

When *or* connects the parts of a compound subject, the verb takes its number from the part of the compound subject closer to it.

Plural

> Either one leek or several onions provide the necessary flavor in most of her recipes. (Because *onions*, a plural, is closer to the verb than *leek*, a singular, the verb must be plural: *provide*.)

When the singular part of the compound subject is closer to the verb, the verb must be singular, as in the following sentence:

Singular

> Neither onions nor garlic is used in this dish.   (The singular *garlic* is closer to the verb, so the verb is singular: *is used*.)

When compound subjects are modified by *each* or *every*, they are always singular. This is true whether *and* or *or* is used to connect the parts of the compound subject.

Consider the following sentences:

Singular

> *Each* boy and girl *is bringing* a friend.
> *Every* boy and girl *is bringing* a friend.
> *Each* boy or girl *is bringing* a friend.
> *Every* boy or girl *is bringing* a friend.

When only one part of a compound subject is modified by *each* or *every*, the compound is a plural.

Plural

> *Each boy and his date are bringing* presents.
> *Every boy and his date are bringing* presents.

13. In the following sentences, supply the correct *form of the verb* as shown in these examples:

> An apple and an orange (be) in every lunch box.   ___are___
> Pie or cake (be) the perfect dessert after such a meal.   ___is___
> Neither Kate nor her friends (play) the piano.   ___play___
> Every boy and girl alive (be) either a little Liberal or else a little Conservative.   ___is___

1. Salami and eggs (be) my favorite dish. _____
2. Spokane and Takoma (be) in the State of Washington. _____
3. Neither Alfred nor Fred (want) to be present when the bill arrives. _____
4. Either Lucy or her father (carve) the turkey at our house. _____
5. Neither goats nor sheep (allow) to graze now in the upper pasture. _____
6. Either Anne or her brothers (be) welcome here. _____
7. All good sons and daughters (take) their turns at doing the dishes. _____
8. A pound of potatoes (go) far when all the children have left home. _____
9. Three carrots and one parsnip (be) all you need to complete the stew. _____
10. Two thick lamb chops or one small steak (feed) our little family. _____
11. One duck and three geese (swim) in our pond every morning. _____
12. Twelve votes for or one vote against (be) all we need for an acceptable decision. _____
13. One bus and three taxi cabs (stand) ready to take the delegates to the meeting. _____
14. The employees and their elected leader (agree) on the terms of the contract. _____
15. Strawberries and cream (be) all I want to eat today. _____
16. Every man and woman (have) a single vote. _____
17. Every edition of the New Testament (have) admirers and attackers. _____
18 He praised most of the television plays and movies that (produced) last year. _____
19. Flowers or cards (comfort) the bereaved. _____
20. Each member of the group and their friends (carry) part of the load. _____

Collective Nouns and Their Verbs

A collective noun takes a *singular* verb when the noun refers to a group *as a unit*. A collective noun takes a *plural* verb when the noun refers individually to the *members of a group*.

Consider the following sentences:

> A married *couple is treated* differently from the way in which a husband or wife is treated alone. (The collective noun *couple* is made up of two people, but they are considered a single unit in this sentence. Since *couple* is singular, the correct verb form is singular: *is treated*.)
>
> The *couple were living* in our neighborhood at that time, so we saw much of *them*. (The collective noun *couple* is considered to be two separate individuals in this sentence. The plural pronoun *them* emphasizes the plurality of *couple*.)
>
> The *class was given its* assignment. (The collective noun *class* is treated as a single unit, so the verb is singular: *was given*. The pronoun *its* emphasizes the singularity of *class*.)

As is apparent, then, the writer must decide the meaning he or she intends in a collective noun and must then be consistent in the use of verbs and pronouns that relate to that collective noun.

The writer must resist the temptation to treat as singular all collective nouns that have the appearance of singulars—*audience, class, group*. The writer must also resist the temptation to treat as plurals all collective nouns that have the appearance of plurals—*athletics, politics, statistics*.

Finally, the writer must remember that collective nouns that are singular in appearance can also be made plural—*audience, audiences; class, classes; group, groups*. When they are made plural in this way, they have different meanings and are treated as plurals.

14. In the following sentences, *supply* the correct *form of the verb* as shown in these examples:

> The board always (vote) the way its leaders tells it to vote. ___votes___
>
> Athletics (be) one of her great interests when she was an undergraduate. ___was___
>
> The majority (realize) that in many ways they have no more power than the smallest minorities. ___realize___

1. He says that his committee (expect) to vote tomorrow. _____
2. The minority always (vote) with a single voice. _____
3. Politics (make) strange bedfellows, but so do many other human enterprises. _____
4. While a number (be) defecting, many others will stay behind. _____
5. The team (work) well as a unit and will probably win most of its matches. _____
6. An American crowd (leave) most of its garbage behind once it has dispersed. _____
7. Committees often (have) no other function than to meet and issue useless reports. _____
8. The contents of my wife's purse always (amaze) me. _____
9. The table of contents (be) never omitted from our company reports. _____
10. A dozen (be) much too expensive for my poor pocketbook. _____

PERSON

Person is the characteristic of verbs that indicates the speaker (*first person*), the person spoken to (*second person*), and the person spoken of (*third person*). Personal pronouns also have the characteristic of *person*.

	Singular	Plural
First Person	I call	We call
Second Person	You call	You call
Third Person	He, she, or it calls	They call

15. In the following sentences, indicate the *person* and *number* of each of the *italicized verbs* as shown in these examples:

Thoreau *is* a favorite of intelligent young people.   third person singular

Even strangers *smile* at the child.   third person plural

We *cannot condone* such outrageous behavior.   first person plural

1. Dick and Lucy *were* good friends. _____
2. Your mother and father *will be* welcome for dinner. _____
3. *Can* you *find* your way alone? _____
4. Michael and I *will be looking* for rooms. _____
5. We *return* on the day after Labor Day. _____
6. They *decided* against supporting us. _____
7. You never *achieve* all the goals you set. _____
8. I *shall be calling you* one day soon after I return. _____
9. Cows *provide* milk and cream. _____
10. Books *have been* his best friends. _____

TENSE

Tense is the characteristic of verbs that indicates the time of the action or of the state of being that is described. There are six tenses in English: *present, past perfect, past, present perfect, future,* and *future perfect.* The *progressive* forms of these tenses indicate ongoing action.

Tense	Present	Past Perfect	Past
	(present action, habitual action, simple future action, action true for all time)	(action completed before a previous past action)	(action completed in the past)
Active Voice	I call	I had called	I called
	You call	You had called	You called
	He calls	He had called	He called
	We call	We had called	We called
	You call	You had called	You called
	They call	They had called	They called

Tense	Present	Past Perfect	Past
Passive Voice	I am called You are called He is called We are called You are called They are called	I had been called You had been called He had been called We had been called You had been called They had been called	I was called You were called He was called We were called You were called They were called
Progressive Active	I am calling You are calling He is calling We are calling You are calling They are calling	I had been calling You had been calling He had been calling We had been calling You had been calling They had been calling	I was calling You were calling He was calling We were calling You were calling They were calling
Progressive Passive (exists only in *present* and *past*)	I am being called You are being called He is being called We are being called You are being called They are being called		I was being called You were being called He was being called We were being called You were being called They were being called

	Present Perfect (action begun in the past that continues in the present)	**Future** (simple future action)	**Future Perfect** (action completed before a future action)
Active Voice	I have called You have called He has called We have called You have called They have called	I will call You will call He will call We will call You will call They will call	I will have called You will have called He will have called We will have called You will have called They will have called
Passive Voice	I have been called You have been called He has been called We have been called You have been called They have been called	I will be called You will be called He will be called We will be called You will be called They will be called	I will have been called You will have been called He will have been called We will have been called You will have been called They will have been called
Progressive Active	I have been calling You have been calling He has been calling We have been calling You have been calling They have been calling	I will be calling You will be calling He will be calling We will be calling You will be calling They will be calling	I will have been calling You will have been calling He will have been calling We will have been calling You will have been calling They will have been calling

16. In the following sentences, indicate the *tense* and *voice* of each of the *italicized verbs* as shown in these examples:

Shakespeare *continues* to interest scholars.   ___present, active___

The plays of Shakespeare *have continued* to interest scholars.   ___present perfect, active___

Many plays of Shakespeare *are produced* each year.   ___present, passive___

1. Research and teaching *supplement* and *reinforce* one another. _____

2. Compliments *have been exchanged* regularly by political friends and enemies alike. _____

3. They *find* private enterprise in its unregulated form still possible today. _____

4. They *have been calling* for justice for all men and women. _____

5. Ian *will be* forty years old next year. _____

6. The minister surely *will be calling* on you soon. _____

7. Many *are called*, but few *are chosen*. _____

8. Many National Guardsmen *are being called* to active duty. _____

9. You *will* soon *find* yourself in even greater peril. _____

10. By the time he *was promoted*, he was old and tired. _____

11. She *had decided* to forgo any further effort on my behalf. _____

12. Architects *are found* only in metropolitan areas. _____

13. Many of the books they *treasured* *had been mutilated*. _____

14. You soon *will receive* your final grades. _____

15. Alice *has failed* to comprehend the true situation. _____

Principal Parts of the Verb

Verbs form their various tenses from their four *principal parts*: the infinitive (*call*), present participle (*calling*), past tense (*called*), and past participle (*called*). The verb *call* used in these examples is classified as *regular*, because it forms its principal parts by adding *ing* or *ed* to the infinitive. *Regular* verbs are also known as *weak* verbs. Verbs that form their past tense and past participle by a change of vowel in the infinitive are classified as *irregular*, or *strong*, verbs. An example of an irregular verb is *draw*. The principal parts of *draw* are *draw*, *drawing*, *drew*, and *drawn*.

The following is a list of the most common *irregular*, or *strong*, verbs:

Infinitive	Present Participle	Past Tense	Past Participle
arise	arising	arose	arisen
be	being	was	been
bear	bearing	bore	borne (carried)
			born (given birth to)
begin	beginning	began	begun
bid (offer)	bidding	bid	bid
bid (order)	bidding	bade	bidden
bite	biting	bit	bitten, bit
blow	blowing	blew	blown
break	breaking	broke	broken
bring	bringing	brought	brought
burst	bursting	burst	burst
catch	catching	caught	caught
choose	choosing	chose	chosen
come	coming	came	come
dig	digging	dug	dug
dive	diving	dove, dived	dived, dove

Infinitive	Present Participle	Past Tense	Past Participle
do	doing	did	done
draw	drawing	drew	drawn
dream	dreaming	dreamed, dreamt	dreamed, dreamt
drink	drinking	drank	drunk
eat	eating	ate	eaten
fall	falling	fell	fallen
find	finding	found	found
flee	fleeing	fled	fled
fly	flying	flew	flown
forget	forgetting	forgot	forgotten, forgot
freeze	freezing	froze	frozen
get	getting	got	got, gotten
give	giving	gave	given
go	going	went	gone
grow	growing	grew	grown
hang	hanging	hung, hanged	hung, hanged
have	having	had	had
hear	hearing	heard	heard
know	knowing	knew	known
lay	laying	laid	laid
lead	leading	led	led
lend	lending	lent	lent
let	letting	let	let
lie	lying	lay	lain
light	lighting	lighted, lit	lighted, lit
lose	losing	lost	lost
pay	paying	paid	paid
		payed (ropes)	payed (ropes)
plead	pleading	pleaded, pled	pleaded, pled
prove	proving	proved	proven, proved
ride	riding	rode	ridden
ring	ringing	rang, rung	rung
rise	rising	rose	risen
run	running	ran	run
say	saying	said	said
see	seeing	saw	seen
set	setting	set	set
shine	shining	shone, shined	shone, shined
show	showing	showed	shown, showed
shrink	shrinking	shrank, shrunk	shrunk
sing	singing	sang, sung	sung
sink	sinking	sank, sunk	sunk
sit	sitting	sat	sat
slide	sliding	slid	slid
sow	sowing	sowed	sown, sowed
speak	speaking	spoke	spoken
spit	spitting	spat, spit	spit, spat
spring	springing	sprang, sprung	sprung
stand	standing	stood	stood
steal	stealing	stole	stolen
stink	stinking	stank, stunk	stunk

Infinitive	Present Participle	Past Tense	Past Participle
swim	swimming	swam, swum	swum
swing	swinging	swung	swung
take	taking	took	taken
tear	tearing	tore	torn
throw	throwing	threw	thrown
tread	treading	trod	trodden, trod
wake	waking	waked, woke	waked, woke, woken
wear	wearing	wore	worn
weave	weaving	wove, weaved	woven, wove
win	winning	won	won
wind	winding	wound	wound
wring	wringing	wrung	wrung
write	writing	wrote	written

17. In the following sentences, supply the *required verb forms*, as shown in these examples:

> She has (write) a letter to her father every week. _____written_____
>
> I (see) an exciting movie last week. _____saw_____

1. We spent the afternoon (dive) for shells off the reef. _____
2. The horse (run) a strong race, even though it came in second. _____
3. Why did the unripe apple (fall) to the ground? _____
4. The bell tolled mournfully, and the old men and women (wring) their hands. _____
5. I have (show) you all the shoes of your size in the store. _____
6. By evening, the hangman (lead) the patriot to the gallows. _____
7. We have (lay) in a good supply of potatoes. _____
8. Codfish is (eat) all winter. _____
9. You can be sure that they (get) all that was coming to them. _____
10. He (dive) three times trying to reach the automobile. _____
11. Helen (lie) in her bed until noon that day. _____
12. Dorothy (shrink) the dress until it fitted her. _____
13. Savings and Loans have (lend) money unwisely. _____
14. The bells in the tower (ring) for fifteen minutes yesterday. _____
15. We sometimes regret words we have (speak). _____

Selection of Tense

The tense of the verb must indicate the appropriate time of action or state of being described by the verb.

It is worthwhile to review here the six English tenses:

(1) Present tense:

> I *like* you. (present action)
>
> The 747 always *flies* smoothly. (habitual action)
>
> The 8:10 commuter train *leaves* in five minutes. (simple future)
>
> The sun *rises* in the east. (action true for all time)

(2) Past perfect tense—action completed before a previous past action:

   She *had left* by the time I arrived.   (*arrived* is past tense; *had left* is past perfect tense.)

   The dog *had eaten* all the cat's food before I walked into the kitchen.   (*walked* is past tense; *had eaten* is past perfect tense.)

(3) Past tense—action completed in the past:

   The movie *ended* at 9:45.

   Tamara *ate* everything on her plate.

(4) Present perfect tense—action begun in the past that continues in the present:

   The tree *has grown* rapidly since last spring.

   I *have found* myself troubled by some of his actions.

(5) Future tense—simple future action:

   I now *will eat* my dinner.

   The book *will be returned*.

(6) Future perfect tense—action completed before a future action:

   Emily *will have eaten* by the time we leave.   (*leave* indicates future action; *will have eaten* is future perfect.)

   The library *will have closed* before we get there.   (*get* indicates future action; *will have closed* is future perfect.)

18. In the following sentences, supply the appropriate *forms of the verbs* as shown in these examples:

   I (eat) many great meals since arriving in Paris.   ___have eaten___

   Two hours (pass) since you called.   ___have passed___

   The volcano no longer (erupt) regularly.   ___erupts___

   1. Dick (be) forty-seven years old next December.   _____
   2. Pomegranates (eat) by many people in recent years.   _____
   3. The language you speak (hurt) my ears.   _____
   4. Nursing homes (become) a permanent part of our lives once families stopped caring for their older members.   _____
   5. The stores (raise) their prices again and again.   _____
   6. As difficult as it is to believe, she (be) eighty years old.   _____
   7. She never (call) her broker during the business day.   _____
   8. (Be) there any way out of the economic mess we're in?   _____
   9. Cigarettes are harmful to health especially when smokers (inhale).   _____
   10. Hurry, children, the school bus (leave) on time this morning.   _____
   11. By the time the police arrived, the criminal (escape).   _____
   12. By the time the passengers arrive, the ship (leave).   _____
   13. Margaret (learn) to swim when she was three years old.   _____
   14. The earth (turn) continuously on its axis.   _____
   15. Every dog must (have) its day.   _____

Agreement of Tenses

The tense of the verb in the main clause of a sentence determines the tense needed in a subordinate clause.

The time of the principal action or state of being described in a sentence is established by the tense of the verb in the main clause. Since subordinate clauses depend on the main clause, the verb tenses in subordinate clauses must agree logically with the tense of the main verb.

Consider the following sentences:

My dog cries whenever she is hungry.   (The main clause is *My dog cries*. The subordinate clause is *whenever she is hungry*. Since *cries* is present tense, indicating habitual action, *is hungry* must also be present tense.)

He coughed because he smoked so much.   (Past tense *coughed* in main clause, past tense *smoked* in subordinate clause.)

He coughs because he smokes so much.   (Present tense *coughs* in main clause, present tense *smokes* in subordinate clause.)

They will have finished their dinner before we begin to eat our own.   (Future perfect *will have finished* in main clause, present tense *begin* in subordinate clause. The present tense here indicates simple future action. Obviously, the actions of both clauses will begin in the future, but the future action of the main verb *will have finished* will have been completed before *begin to eat*, the second future action, occurs. The verb in the subordinate clause can also be future, *will begin*.)

Thus, in establishing the proper tense of a verb in a subordinate clause, the tense of the main verb must govern, and logic must be used.

19. In the following sentences, supply the *appropriate forms of the verbs* as shown in these examples:

She had decided to go to the country by the time her mother (return).   ___returned___
Once she (make) up her mind, she never changes it.   ___makes___

1. A courtesy car was no longer supplied, even though customers (like) it.   _____
2. Large automobiles did not disappear even though the manufacturers (learn) gasoline economy.   _____
3. Jane found the letter that (deliver) to her secretary.   _____
4. The book was sent in a wrapper that (give) no indication of its contents.   _____
5. I have always eaten spinach because I (like) it.   _____
6. Even though many passengers (miss) the plane, it left the gate on time.   _____
7. As he (watch), most of the children left the bus.   _____
8. While we (wait), many of the guests sat down to eat.   _____
9. Students find their work piling up when the term (come) to a close.   _____
10. They will have completed their jobs by Tuesday, which (be) the scheduled final date for the project.   _____

11. The lecturer emphasized that the Romantic Period (be) rich in poetry. _____

12. Deirdre said that imagination (be) the key to successful fiction. _____

13. Oak leaves stayed on the trees long after winter (arrive). _____

14. When most current plays (act) no more, the works of Ibsen will continue to be popular.

_____

15. Snow remains on the ground in Vermont until spring (be) well under way.

_____

Present Tense for Ideas True for All Time

The present tense is always used when we wish to express ideas that are taken to be true for all time. This holds even in subordinate clauses, regardless of the tense of the main verb.

Consider the following sentences:

He demonstrated once more that truth *is* stranger than fiction.

Freud identified fundamental drives that *are found* in all of us.

The present tense is used in the subordinate clauses of both these sentences: *is* and *are found*. Yet the main clauses have verbs in the past tense: *demonstrated* and *identified*. Were the statements of the subordinate clauses not taken to be true for all time, then the past tense would have been used instead of the present.

Consider the following sentences, in which the statements of the subordinate clauses are not taken to be true for all time:

He demonstrated once more that he was untrustworthy.   (The verb *was* in the past tense is correct, because *demonstrated* is past, and *he* may one day reform and become trustworthy.)

Freud identified the condition that was troubling his patient. (The verb *was troubling* is correctly formed in the past tense, since proper medical treatment can be expected to cure the condition and the condition therefore is not true for all time.)

20. In the following sentences, supply the correct *form of the verb* as shown in these examples:

Peary established that man (be) the master of the Arctic ice. _____is_____

My daughter told me that *Gulliver's Travels* (be) her favorite book in childhood.

_____was_____

1. He found that the endless sand of the desert (be) too much for him. _____

2. Jason found through experience that there (be) more to skiing than having expensive equipment. _____

3. Gloria's speech will emphasize that freedom (entail) responsibility. _____

4. The weather report did not say that we (have) snow tomorrow. _____

5. He intends to take the early flight, which (depart) tomorrow at 9 o'clock. _____

6. Dictionaries usually supply the meanings of all words that students (use).

                                                            _____

7. Engineers and scientists always agreed that the accuracy of the slide rule (be) sufficient for most of their work.   _____

8. The argument that the defendant (be) the slave of his habits did not sway the jury in this case.   _____

9. The lecturer went on at great length to prove that Hardy and Conrad (know) the lives of ordinary people and (portray) those lives accurately.   _____

10. The growing cost of education means that taxes (continue) to increase in the next decade.   _____

CONSISTENCY OF VERBS

Shifts of voice, person, tense, and mood should be avoided within a sentence.

Consistency of Voice

Acceptable

Once I had completed the treatment, I was troubled with pain no longer. (One verb is active, the other passive.)

Improved

Once I had completed the treatment, I experienced no more pain.

Consistency of Person

Incorrect

We should always study when you are fresh. (The main verb *should study* is third person, but the subordinate verb *are* is second person.)

Correct

Students should study when they are fresh. (Both verbs third person.)

Correct

Study whenever you are fresh. (Both verbs second person.)

Consistency of Tense

Incorrect

An actress usuallys studies new roles during the run of a play, even though she was gainfully employed. (Incorrect shift from present tense *studies* to past tense *was employed*. Note too that *studies* is active voice, but *was employed* is passive.)

Correct

An actress usually studies new roles during the run of a play, even though she is working. (Both verbs in present tense, active voice.)

Consistency of Mood

Incorrect

His advice was in two parts: discover what you want to do and then you will find your way toward that goal.   (The verb *discover* is in the imperative mood; the verb *will find* is in the indicative mood.)

Correct

His advice was in two parts: discover what you want to do and then find your way toward that goal.   (Both verbs in imperative mood.)

21. Restructure the following sentences as necessary to achieve consistency of *voice, person, tense,* and *mood,* as shown in these examples:

After I succeeded in overcoming the virus, progress toward general recovery began.

  After I had succeeded in overcoming the virus, I began to recover generally.

Investors often will reinvest in declining stocks, because they were willing to throw good money after bad.

  Investors often will reinvest in declining stocks, because they are willing to throw good money after bad.

1. The first thing to do is remove the wheel, and then you should examine the brakes.

2. Some writers work only four hours a day, because you cannot do creative work for longer periods.

3. They found that they could not sew the seams well, since you always make mistakes when you first try to learn a new skill.

4. When one has little money to spend, you are careful about every purchase.

5. If you go to the dance, one will find unescorted women welcome.

6. Because he considered the design perfect, the judges had ruled against him.

7. Be seated, and the lecturer will tell you all you need to know.

8. He selected the material for the coat, and the tailor is then told to begin work.

9. The women had insisted on admitting men to their group, but most of the men find the meetings dull.

10. Nightmares disturb his sleep night after night, and he will find no relief in sedatives.

VERBALS

Verbals—*infinitives*, *participles*, and *gerunds*—are verb forms that can function as nouns, adjectives, and adverbs.

INFINITIVE

The infinitive is the form of the verb that appears in the dictionary. Outside dictionaries, the infinitive is usually preceded by *to*: *to swim*, *to play*, *to ask*. The infinitive may often appear without *to*, especially after *can*, *do*, *may*, *must*, *shall*, and *will*: *can swing*, *may play*, *must ask*. The infinitive has both tense and voice.

	Active Voice	Passive Voice
Present tense	(to) call, (to) be calling	(to) be called
Perfect tense	(to) have called	(to) have been called
	(to) have been calling	

The infinitive may function as a noun, as an adjective, as an adverb, or as a complement.

Infinitive as Noun

> *To swim* is my greatest pleasure.   (*To swim* is the subject of the verb *is*.)
>
> They asked *to see* the patient.   (*To see* is the object of the verb *asked*.)

Infinitive as Adjective

> Juliet gave me something *to read*.   (*To read* modifies the noun *something*.)
>
> They have a desire *to be saved*.   (*To be saved* modifies the noun *desire*.)

Infinitive as Adverb

> I am happy *to wait*.   (*To wait* modifies the adjective *happy*.)
>
> The baby is heavy enough *to go* home.   (*To go* modifies the adverb *enough*.)

Infinitive as Complement

> Henry's ambition was *to be* a playwright.   (*To be* is the complement of *was*.)
>
> Ambition is *to be expected* in young executives. (*To be expected* is the complement of *is*.)

22. In the following sentences, identify the functions of the *italicized infinitives* as noun, adjective, adverb, or complement as shown in these examples:

> *To teach* well is an art.   ___noun___
>
> She has a cross *to bear*.   ___adjective___
>
> She was content *to take* half the money.   ___adverb___
>
> He is *to be congratulated*.   ___complement___

1. Copies of the Oxford American Dictionary are *to be purchased*.   _____
2. That book is small enough *to be carried* in a vest pocket.   _____
3. She helped him *work* the calculus problem.   _____
4. *To learn* grammar is not easy.   _____

5. They watched us *pour* the wine. _____

6. The seeds are *to be planted* in shallow beds. _____

7. *To have understood* her was my earnest desire. _____

8. The instructor may have *to delay* the final examination. _____

9. Can we expect *to find* happiness? _____

10. He wants *to speak* before the others have a chance. _____

Infinitive Phrases

In some sentences, the infinitive itself has a subject, object or complement, and modifiers.

Such a construction is called an *infinitive phrase*, and it may function as subject, object, complement, or modifier of another sentence element.

Consider the following sentences:

To mow the entire lawn required three strong boys. (The infinitive phrase *To mow the entire lawn* is the subject of the verb *required*. Within the infinitive phrase, *lawn* is the object of *to mow*. *The entire* modifies *lawn*.)

Catherine hoped *to row the choppy lake*. (The infinitive phrase *to row the choppy lake* is the object of *hoped*. Within the infinitive phrase, *lake* is the object of *to row*, *the choppy* modifies *lake*.)

Deirdre is *to marry next year*. (The infinitive phrase *to marry next year* is the complement of the copulative verb *is*. Within the infinitive phrase, *next year* modifies *to marry*, and *next* modifies *year*.)

They have enough firewood *to last the winter*. (The infinitive phrase *to last the winter* modifies *enough*. Within the infinitive phrase, *winter* is the object of *to last*. *The* modifies *winter*.)

They wanted *the instructor to submit his grades promptly*. (The infinitive phrase *the instructor to submit his grades promptly* is the object of *wanted*. Within the infinitive phrase, *instructor* is the subject of *to submit*, *grades* is the object of *to submit*, *his* modifies *grades*, and *promptly* modifies *to submit*.)

23. In the following sentences, underline each *infinitive phrase*, identify *its function*, and identify the *function of each word within the phrase* as shown in these examples:

Fred wanted me to buy snowshoes immediately.

Function of phrase	object of *wanted*
Functions of words	*me* subject of *to buy*, *snowshoes* object of *to buy*, *immediately* modifies *to buy*

To judge by her skeptical nature, she must have had some unfaithful friends.

Function of phrase	modifies *she*
Functions of words	*by her skeptical nature* modifies *to judge*, *by* introduces prepositional phrase, *her skeptical* modifies *nature*, *nature* is object of preposition *by*

1. The company executive ordered the employees to complete the job on schedule.
        Function of phrase   _____
        Functions of words   _____
                              _____

2. To identify enemies, the President met with the National Security Council.
        Function of phrase   _____
        Functions of words   _____
                              _____

3. Alex told her to forget her achievements completely.
        Function of phrase   _____
        Functions of words   _____
                              _____

4. She asked me to answer the phone in her absence.
        Function of phrase   _____
        Functions of words   _____
                              _____

5. To achieve his ambition required hard work.
        Function of phrase   _____
        Functions of words   _____
                              _____

Tenses of the Infinitive

The present infinitive is used if its action occurs *at the same time as* the action of the main verb or *after* the action of the main verb. The perfect infinitive is used if its action *precedes* that of the main verb.

	Active	**Passive**
Present	(to) tell, (to) be telling	(to) be told
Perfect	(to) have told, (to) have been telling	(to) have been told

Consider the following sentences:

> She does not want *to continue* the conversation.
>
> She did not want *to continue* the conversation.

In each of these sentences, the present infinitive *to continue* is used, because its action occurs either, in the first example, *at the same time as* or, in the second example, *after the action of* the main verb.

> It is senseless *to have told* such a story.

In this sentence, the main verb *is* is in the present tense. The writer of the sentence is stating something he or she believes to be true now and forever. Yet the action that was considered *senseless* occurred before this statement was made. For this reason, the perfect infinitive *to have told* is used.

> It was senseless *to tell* such a story.

The meaning intended here is that telling the story was senseless at the time the story was told. Because the action described by the infinitive occurred at the same time as the action of the main verb, the present infinitive *to tell* is used.

24. In the following sentences, supply the correct *form of the infinitive* as shown in these examples:

> There was no way possible (consume) all that food in one sitting.   <u>to have consumed</u>
> He decided (reveal) the whole truth.   <u>to reveal</u>

1. How could he have been stupid enough (take) such a position on an issue so grave?

   _____

2. There will be time enough (forgive) those who bolted the party. _____
3. He is inclined (delay) payment at least for one more month. _____
4. The elephants ought (feed) now by the keepers. _____
5. The rhinoceroses ought (feed) hours ago. _____
6. Can you think of any gentle way for us (tell) them the details of the ugly incident?

   _____

7. I was unable (tell) them all the facts of the case. _____
8. They intend (play) fair with their opponents. _____
9. He is reluctant (admit) that he intentionally ruined their chances. _____
10. Everyone agreed it was difficult (prepare) for such an examination. _____

Split Infinitives

An infinitive should not be split when the result is awkward.

English teachers and grammarians may have overstressed the idea of keeping the parts of an infinitive together. Such an approach to style probably stems from Latin grammar. In Latin, the infinitive never employs the preposition *to*, so there is no possibility of splitting an infinitive. In English, however, too strict compliance with the advice never to split an infinitive may result in awkward constructions. At the same time, splitting an infinitive with lengthy phrases or clauses may also result in awkwardness.

You recall that the infinitive has the following forms:

	Active	**Passive**
Present	(to) find, (to) be finding	(to) be found
Perfect	(to) have found, (to) have been finding	(to) have been found

Consider the following examples of good infinitive constructions, awkward infinitive constructions, and impossible infinitive constructions:

Good

> *To think* clearly on her feet was her goal.   (*Clearly* modifies *to think*.)

Awkward

> *To clearly think* at all times was her goal.   (This construction is awkward because *clearly* appears to modify *think* rather than *to think*.)

Impossible

> *To* clearly at all times *think* was her goal.

Good

> They hoped *to find* the child quickly.

Awkward

> They hoped *to* quickly *find* the child.

Good

> They see no need *to be thinking* day after day about the problems they face.

Impossible

> They see no need *to be*, day after day *thinking* about the problems they face.

In some cases, a construction may be awkward because care has been taken not to split an infinitive. Consider the following sentences:

Awkward

> Their advice was *to double* more than our energies.   (This sentence makes no sense at all. What else besides *energies* were we supposed *to double*?)

Good

> Their advice was *to* more than *double* our energies.   (By placing the modifier *more than* in the midst of the infinitive, the sentence has some meaning.)

Modifiers can generally be placed in more than one position in a sentence. The writer must seek the best position for modifiers, remembering that long modifiers that split infinitives almost always result in awkward constructions.

25.   In the following sentences, underscore and correct any *awkward infinitive constructions* as shown in these examples:

> The advice of the doctors was <u>to moderately eat.</u>
> _____to eat moderately_____
> She made it a rule <u>to never hurriedly eat</u> her meals.
> ___to never eat her meals hurriedly_ *or* never to eat her meals hurriedly___

1.   They expect to more than lose a million dollars.

   _____

2.   To relax and think quietly was her habit most afternoons.

   _____

3.   To more than two hours work overtime in a day is against company policy.

   _____

4.   After the game, the team was instructed to not board the bus for the trip home.

   _____

5.   The hope of the search party was to safe and sound find the child before darkness set in.

   _____

6.   She has decided to firmly but respectfully demand that her husband be hired.

   _____

7. To have within an hour walked around the park was impossible.

_____

8. There was nothing worthwhile left to do under the circumstances.

_____

9. He decided to without hesitation tell the entire story.

_____

10. The Smiths were impatient to without delay sell their car.

_____

PARTICIPLE

Participles are verbal adjectives that have present and past tenses: *calling*, *called*. When participles are combined with auxiliary verbs—*I am calling*, *she has called*, etc.—they indicate tense (see page 70) and do not function as adjectives. Consider the following:

Laughing at us, he threw us a quarter.   (*Laughing* modifies *he*. It is the condition *he* is in when he performs the action of throwing. *Laughing* is modified by the prepositional phrase *at us*.)

The actor left the room, *crying* happily and *throwing* kisses at us all.   (*Crying* and *throwing* modify *actor*. They describe the condition the actor was in when leaving the room. *Crying* is modified by *happily*. *Kisses* is the direct object of *throwing*. *At us all* modifies *throwing*.)

The *annoying* child finally left the dining room.   (*Annoying* modifies *child*.)

Having received my termination notice, I packed up all my belongings and left the office. (*Having received* modifies *I*.)

Sustained for more than an hour by her life belt, she made her way to shore.   (*Sustained* modifies *she*.)

26. In the following sentences, underline the *participles* and identify the *word* or *words they modify* as shown in these examples:

The book relied on most by writers is the dictionary.   _____book_____

Having written another best-selling novel, she was able to take an extended vacation.

_____she_____

1. Rushing through both rooms, Christopher slammed the door. _____

2. Having been told the news, Hillary quietly left the room.   _____

3. Found money most often is spent foolishly. _____

4. Sustained by my faith, I shall go on as though nothing happened. _____

5. A child locked in a room will find mischief. _____

6. Swallowing hurriedly, the older boy reached for the rifle. _____

7. Left on her own, Felice began to mature. _____

8. Having refused the second offer, William had little chance of keeping negotiations open.

_____

9. Tired by the long argument, the attorney found herself unable to continue.

_____

10. Congratulating her opponent, Hingis left the court. _____

Tenses of the Participle

The present participle is used to indicate action occurring at the same time as the action of the main verb. The past participle is used to indicate action prior to the action of the main verb.

	Active	**Passive**
Present	telling	being told
Past	having told	told, having been told

Consider the following sentences:

> *Telling* the story as well as he could, he knew it would not be believed.
> *Having told* the story as well as he could, he sat down.

In the first sentence, the subject of the sentence knows as he is telling the story that *it would not be believed*. The present participle *telling* is used, because the action of the participle is occurring at the same time as the action of the verb *knew*. In the second sentence, the action of the participle *having told* precedes the past action of the main verb *sat*. For this reason, the past participle is used.

27. In the following sentences, supply the correct *form of the participle* as shown in these examples:

> (stare) at me severely, the child refused to answer.
>
>   _____Staring_____
>
> (conclude) her summation of the evidence, the defense attorney rested her client's case.
>
>   _____Having concluded_____

1. (tell) he was no longer needed, he decided to ask for a transfer.

   _____

2. (find) the door closed behind her, she looks about for an emergency exit.

   _____

3. (leave) the Army with an honorable discharge, she was surprised that it took three months to find a job that would pay a living wage.

   _____

4. (refuse) the honorary degree, the physicist did his best to justify his behavior.

   _____

5. (offer) the house for $5000 less than its market value, the couple expected to sell it quickly.

   _____

6. Customers (arrive) after six o'clock will find the store closed.

   _____

7. The auditors will be concerned with entries (omit) from the books.

   _____

8. Our new dean will find the new position (challenge).

   _____

9. Not (realize) your problem was that difficult, I wonder why you were so long in arriving at a reasonable solution.

   _____

10. (retire) from the stage, my wife is often called on to perform without pay.

    _____

GERUND

A *gerund* is the *-ing* form of a verb used as a noun.

A gerund may function as the *subject* or *object* of a verb or as the *object of a preposition*:

> Dialing is no longer necessary.   (The gerund *dialing* is the subject of the verb *is*.)
> She still likes boxing.   (The gerund *boxing* is the object of the verb *likes*.)
> He is given to equivocating.   (*Equivocating* is the object of the preposition *to*.)
> This porch is used only for sunning.   (*Sunning* is the object of the preposition *for*.)

A gerund may also function as a complement, may be modified, and may take an object:

> My favorite hobby is gardening.   (*Gardening* is the complement of *is*.)
> My new interest is organic gardening.   (*Gardening* is modified by the adjective *organic*.)
> Your future depends on working vigorously toward a realistic goal.   (*Working* is modified by the adverb *vigorously*.)
> Hoarding groceries in times of shortages leads to greater shortages.   (*Hoarding* has as its object the noun *groceries*.)

28. In the following sentences, identify the *functions*, *modifiers*, and *objects*, if any, of the italicized *gerunds*. Remember that a gerund may function as the subject of a verb, object of a verb, object of a preposition, or complement. If a gerund is modified, the modifier is either an adjective or adverb. Use the following examples as guides:

> Hours of dull *editing* proved too much to take.

Function	object of preposition
Modifiers	adjective *dull*
Object	none

> Economic *forecasting* is far from precise.

Function	subject of verb
Modifiers	adjective *economic*
Object	none

> *Swallowing* food hastily can lead to disaster.

Function	subject of verb
Modifiers	adverb *hastily*
Object	food

1. *Plowing* was hard work when a man had to depend on an animal instead of a tractor.

       Function   _____

       Modifiers   _____

       Object   _____

2. He found *cooking* interesting for a while.

       Function   _____

       Modifiers   _____

       Object   _____

3. For relaxing, Mr. Churchill often turned to *painting*.

       Function   _____

       Modifiers   _____

       Object   _____

4. He also enjoyed *bricklaying* from time to time.

       Function   _____

       Modifiers   _____

       Object   _____

5. Her principal occupation was *finding* enough to eat.

       Function   _____

       Modifiers   _____

       Object   _____

6. *Preparing* specimens for dissection is not enjoyable before lunch.

       Function   _____

       Modifiers   _____

       Object   _____

7. *Cutting* quickly to the bone helped the surgeon find the source of the infection that threatened the patient's life.

       Function   _____

       Modifiers   _____

       Object   _____

8. *Writing* scholarly papers rapidly is not as important as writing them well.

       Function   _____

       Modifiers   _____

       Object   _____

9. Good *writing* is not easy to find.

       Function   _____

       Modifiers   _____

       Object   _____

10. I found his *writing* tedious.

       Function   _____

       Modifiers   _____

       Object   _____

VERBALS USED AS MODIFIERS

Participles and infinitives are verbals that are used as modifiers. Like all modifiers, they must be clearly identified with the words they modify.

Consider the following sentences:

Driving from the tee, the golfer scored his first birdie.   (The participle *driving* modifies the noun *golfer*.)

Having served the same general for six years, the soldier knew all his habits.   (The participle *having served* modifies the noun *soldier*.)

The teeming rain flooded suburban streets.   (The participle *teeming* modifies *rain*.)

The grocer telephoned the wholesaler to order additional supplies.   (The infinitive *to order* modifies the verb *telephoned*, so *to order* functions as an adverb.)

Mary had an assignment to complete.   (The infinitive *to complete* modifies the noun *assignment*, so *to complete* functions as an adjective.)

DANGLING AND MISPLACED MODIFIERS

Modifiers not clearly identified with words they modify are called *dangling modifiers* or *misplaced modifiers*.

Dangling Participles

Having eaten Chinese food many times before, there was no reason to become ill.   (*Having eaten* is a participle that is part of the participial phrase *Having eaten Chinese food many times before*. The entire phrase acts as a modifier, but has nothing to modify in the principal clause *there was no reason to become ill*. The phrase, therefore, is considered a dangling modifier.)

The sentence is repaired by supplying a noun, pronoun, or noun phrase for the participle to modify:

Correct

Having eaten Chinese food many times before, I had no reason to become ill.

Another way to repair the sentence is to convert the participial phrase into a dependent clause:

Correct

Since I had eaten Chinese food many times before, I had no reason to become ill.

Correct

Since I had eaten Chinese food many times before, there was no reason for me to become ill.

Misplaced Participles

Even when modifiers have a noun, pronoun, or noun phrase to modify, a writer may mislead readers if a modified element is not clearly identifiable. Such a modifier is classified as a misplaced modifier. The construction is faulty and must be corrected.

Consider the following sentence:

Swimming as fast as possible, I saw the boy ahead of me.   (Who was swimming as fast as possible—*the boy* or *I*?)

Correct

I saw the boy ahead of me, swimming as fast as possible.   (It was *the boy*.)

Correct

I swam as fast as possible and finally saw the boy ahead of me.   (It was *I*.)

Dangling Infinitives

Thus far the discussion has centered on dangling and misplaced participles. But what is true for participles is also true for infinitives.

Consider the following sentence:

To convey information, the reader must be considered.   (*To convey information* does not modify anything in the sentence.)

Correct

To convey information, the writer must consider the reader.

Correct

A writer who wishes to convey information must consider the reader.

29. In the following sentences, correct the *dangling* and *misplaced modifiers* as shown in these examples:

Stretching across the yard, I saw a clothesline.
<u>I saw a clothesline stretching across the yard.</u>
After showing my pass, the gate immediately opened.
<u>After I had shown my pass, the gate opened immediately.</u>
To reach my office by 8:15, the train must be on time.
<u>The train must be on time if I am to reach my office by 8:15.</u>

1. To sell that many automobiles, a great many people must like the design.

2. Standing in the runway, a plane will hit somebody.

3. Having run for many weeks, I considered the play a success.

4. Before gaining admittance to his apartment, a bell must be rung.

5. Having helped the old man cross the street, the rest of the walk was uneventful.

6. To achieve even modest acceptance, all aspects of the painting must be considered carefully.

7.   To win over a hostile audience, the performers must be at their best.

_____

8.   Stumbling blindly in the fog, I saw a man appear.

_____

9.   Having assembled all the necessary ingredients, a fine dinner is certain.

_____

10.   To prepare a fine dinner, all ingredients must be fresh.

_____

AUXILIARY VERBS AND INFINITIVES IN COMPOUND CONSTRUCTIONS

Auxiliary Verbs

When different tenses are used within a compound construction, the auxiliary verbs must usually be supplied in full. When the same tense is used throughout a compound construction, repetition of the auxiliary verbs is not usually necessary.

Consider the following sentences:

> Basketball *has become* and always *will be* the favorite sport of Americans.   (The first part of the compound verb is in the perfect *has become*. The second part is in the future *will be*. Because the two tenses are different, the auxiliary verbs *has* and *will* must be supplied.)

> All the players will be given uniforms if they *have studied* hard and *practiced* regularly. (Note that *have* is not needed before *practiced*, because *have studied* and [have] *practiced* are both in the perfect tense.)

Infinitives

In compound constructions employing infinitives, *to* can be used before each infinitive to emphasize the parallel structure.

> She was told *to submit* her application promptly and *to report* for a full physical examination.

The second *to* can be omitted if emphasis is not desirable:

> She was told *to submit* her application promptly and *report* for a full physical examination.

In a series employing infinitives, the first infinitive is always preceded by *to*. If the second infinitive is also preceded by *to*, then all the rest must be preceded by *to*. In most series, however, the initial *to* is usually sufficient.

Consider the following sentences:

Correct

> She was told to *submit* her application, *report* for a physical examination, and *present* suitable references from recent employers.

Correct

> She was told *to submit* her application, *to report* for a physical examination, and *to present* references from her recent employers.

Incorrect

> She was told *to submit* her application, *to report* for a physical examination, and *present* suitable references from recent employers.   (The sentence can be corrected by deleting the *to* before *report* or by inserting *to* before *present*.)

30. Where appropriate in the following sentences, supply all necessary parts of the *verbs* and *infinitives* as shown in these examples:

> She loves to swim, to skate, and <u>fish</u>.
>
> ___to fish___
> _____
>
> Many of the new nations of Africa have been struggling to ensure that their populations will have employment and that their economic goals <u>been met</u> by the end of the next decade.
>
> ___will have been met___
> _____
>
> The various community groups are joining forces to demand equal treatment of men and women, to increase welfare payments for the needy, and <u>establish</u> day care centers for the children of working parents.
>
> ___to establish___
> _____

1. The firefighters must be given sufficient free time to regain their strength and repair their equipment.

   _____

2. Teachers report that all the children they teach have been under strain and going to do badly on citywide achievement tests.

   _____

3. Books are said to comfort the bereaved, inspire the young, and guide the perplexed.

   _____

4. Reading Scripture is said to comfort the invalid and guide the student.

   _____

5. They have been training for the expedition all year and leaving by January.

   _____

6. Job applications are available for distribution to those who have passed the qualifying examination and now desire employment.

   _____

7. Applications will be given only to those who have passed the examination and willing to take jobs immediately.

   _____

8. The couple decided to abandon their life in the country, to sell their possessions, and take an apartment in the city.

   _____

9. Large houses have been and continue to be difficult to sell these days.

   _____

10. Seal hunting has always been considered inhumane, but men continue to hunt these beautiful animals, skinning them alive and to leave their dying bodies behind to be eaten by scavenging birds.

PARALLEL STRUCTURE AND VERB FORMS

Parallel structure must be preserved in sentences using two or more verbs or verbals.

Parallel grammatical constructions are used to express parallel ideas. This means that compound constructions must contain grammatically identical forms. This requirement is especially important for verbs and verbals. (It is easy to recognize a compound construction by the presence of a coordinating conjunction: *and*, *bit*, *or*, *nor*.)

Consider the following sentences:

Correct

I often *swim*, *fish*, and *hunt*.   (The three verbs are in identical form, the present indicative.)

Incorrect

I like *swimming*, *fishing*, and *to hunt*.   (In the series, *swimming* and *fishing* are gerunds; *to hunt* is an infinitive. The structure is not parallel.)

Correct

I like *swimming*, *fishing*, and *hunting*.   (Three gerunds.)

I like to *swim*, *fish*, and *hunt*.   (Three infinitives.)

Correct

Paradoxically, the helicopter has been used *to save* lives and *to take* lives.   (Two infinitives.)

The coach stressed two ideas: *play* hard and *win*.   (*Play* and *win* both imperative, second person.)

The coach stressed two ideas: *playing* hard and *winning*.   (Two participles modifying *ideas*.)

Incorrect

The coach stressed two ideas: *play* hard and *winning*.   (The imperative *play* is incorrectly combined with the participle *winning*.)

31. In the following sentences, underline the *mistakes in parallel construction* and correct them, as shown in these examples:

Marianne Moore was an outstanding American poet, loved baseball, and a <u>Dodger fan.</u>

      <u>was a Dodger fan</u>

When jobs are hard to find, people who want a job must look for work constantly, keep their spirits up, and be alert to every opportunity.

      <u>correct</u>

1. Poor direction by management can cause employees to make many mistakes and creating poor morale.

2. Rhododendrons should not be planted in northern climates or be cultivated closely.

   _____

3. He admires good books, loves classical music, and adores beautiful women.

   _____

4. Neither borrowing nor to lend will lead to happiness.

   _____

5. She spent her days peacefully, but she was finding that the evenings dragged.

   _____

6. The President's goal is to help other nations and preserving the independence of her own people.

   _____

7. Blending an acceptable spaghetti sauce and cooking it properly are easy tasks even for a novice cook.

   _____

8. Ketchup is an all-purpose food disguise, capable of masking the worst in a meat loaf and to ruin the best scrambled eggs.

   _____

9. Harry shattered the window and then went right to his father to ask forgiveness.

   _____

10. Commencement exercises seemed to Jack both a bore and annoying.

    _____

CHAPTER 4

Pronouns

A pronoun is a word or words used in place of a noun, a noun and its modifiers, or another pronoun. The element replaced is called the *antecedent* of the pronoun.

Consider the following sentences:

Secrecy characterizes every action of the leading political parties. *It* is accepted unquestioningly by the voters.   (The word *It* substitutes for *Secrecy*. The noun *Secrecy* in the first sentence is the antecedent of the pronoun *It*.)

The voters in our town voted against the bond issue. *They* vowed to vote no additional funds.   (*They* substitutes for the noun *voters* and its modifier *in our town*. *The voters in our town* in the first sentence is the antecedent of *They*.)

She baked bread so well that *her* customers bought exclusively from *her*.   (*her* and *her* are pronouns with the common antecedent *She*.)

Larry worked so well that his boss promoted *him*.   (*him* is a pronoun with the antecedent *Larry*.)

1. In the following sentences, identify the *pronouns* and their *antecedents* as shown in these examples:

John gave the money to Jane. He gave the money to her.

Pronoun	He; her
Antecedent	John; Jane

Deirdre balanced her checkbook. She then deposited additional funds.

Pronoun	her; she
Antecedent	Deirdre; Deirdre

1. Kate and Leonard saved regularly for the house they knew they would purchase one day.

Pronoun	
Antecedent	

2. The dog chased the mouse and finally killed it.

      Pronoun   _____

      Antecedent _____

3. The painter prepared five brushes, and he finally got to use them.

      Pronoun   _____

      Antecedent _____

      Pronoun   _____

      Antecedent _____

4. Heinrich Böll was awarded the Nobel Prize for Literature after he had achieved worldwide recognition for his work.

      Pronoun   _____

      Antecedent _____

5. Long after he had returned to civilian life, the war veteran found he was still anxious from time to time.

      Pronoun   _____

      Pronoun   _____

      Antecedent _____

6. John and Sally worked hard together. He did the physical labor, and she did the clerical work.

      Pronoun   _____

      Antecedent _____

      Pronoun   _____

      Antecedent _____

7. John and Sally worked hard together. They shared the work fairly. She did the physical labor, and he attended to the records.

      Pronoun   _____

      Antecedent _____

      Pronoun   _____

      Antecedent _____

      Pronoun   _____

      Antecedent _____

8. The children found their game tiresome. It consisted of nothing more than repeating a few words over and over until they were memorized.

      Pronoun   _____

      Antecedent _____

      Pronoun   _____

      Antecedent _____

9. Joan and Audrey found they were working more harmoniously than they had expected.

      Pronoun   _____

      Pronoun   _____

      Antecedent _____

10. Teachers and parents agreed that they had the same interests.

    Pronoun   _____

    Antecedent   _____

11. Extraction of a wisdom tooth can cause great pain if it is impacted.

    Pronoun   _____

    Antecedent   _____

12. The governor signed the proclamation even though she did not understand the reasons why it was drafted.

    Pronoun   _____

    Antecedent   _____

    Pronoun   _____

    Antecedent   _____

13. Zebras are prized for the beauty they display.

    Pronoun   _____

    Antecedent   _____

14. Mr. Cunningham is known for music lessons of quality. They have a liveliness of their own that he never fails to communicate.

    Pronoun   _____

    Antecedent   _____

    Pronoun   _____

    Antecedent   _____

15. Dan told his son that he would be given a watch that would help him get home on time.

    Pronoun   _____

    Pronoun   _____

    Pronoun   _____

    Antecedent   _____

16. Textbooks cost money, but they are worth it.

    Pronoun   _____

    Antecedent   _____

17. Mary left all the dishes in the sink, even though she knew she would have to do them when she returned from the movies.

    Pronoun   _____

    Pronoun   _____

    Pronoun   _____

    Antecedent   _____

    Pronoun   _____

    Antecedent   _____

18. Marjorie's mother gave her a bracelet to wear when she attended the party.

    Pronoun   _____

    Pronoun   _____

    Antecedent   _____

19. The doctor will test Jon again when he is five years old.

     Pronoun   _____

     Antecedent _____

20. Ruth is bound to sell some antiques if she tries long enough.

     Pronoun   _____

     Antecedent _____

21. San Francisco has its advantages, but they cost tourists dearly when they are not careful.

     Pronoun   _____

     Antecedent _____

     Pronoun   _____

     Antecedent _____

22. Two atomic bombs ended World War II, and they are still remembered today.

     Pronoun   _____

     Antecedent _____

23. Vermont imposes heavy income taxes when it needs funds.

     Pronoun   _____

     Antecedent _____

24. In a democracy, citizens have equal rights, but not all of them exercise their rights.

     Pronoun   _____

     Pronoun   _____

     Antecedent _____

25. Chicago is a beautiful city, but it lacks proximity to New York.

     Pronoun   _____

     Antecedent _____

TYPES OF PRONOUNS

There are many types of pronouns. The most important are *personal, impersonal, relative, demonstrative, interrogative, reflexive, intensive, reciprocal,* and *indefinite*. As a first step in learning these terms, examine the following examples of each type:

Personal pronouns: *I, you, he, she, we, they, one*
Impersonal pronouns: *it, they*
Relative pronouns: *who, which, that, whoever, whichever*
Demonstrative pronouns: *this, that, these, those*
Interrogative pronouns: *who, which, what, whoever, whatever*
Reflexive pronouns: *myself, yourself, himself, herself, ourselves, yourselves, themselves, itself*
Intensive pronouns: *myself, yourself, himself, herself, ourselves, yourselves, themselves, itself*
Reciprocal pronouns: *each other, one another*
Indefinite pronouns: *each, either, any, anyone, some, someone, all*

Personal and Impersonal Pronouns

Personal pronouns refer to people. *Impersonal* pronouns refer to everything but people.

Personal and impersonal pronouns can be *singular* or *plural*. They can also be in the *subjective, possessive,* or *objective case*. Personal pronouns may also indicate *gender*.

The following table summarizes *personal* and *impersonal* pronouns in number, case, and gender:

	Subjective	**Possessive**	**Objective**
First person			
Singular	I	mine	ours
Plural	we	ours	us
Second person			
Singular	you	yours	you
Plural	you	yours	you
Third person			
Singular			
Masculine	he	his	him
Feminine	she	hers	her
Neuter	it	its	it
Any gender	one	one's	one
Plural			
All genders	they	theirs	them

The following sentences illustrate the uses of personal and impersonal pronouns in each of the three cases:

Subjective Case

    I (We, You, They) see the entire scene.

    He (She, It, One) sees the entire scene.

Possessive Case (See pages 103–104 for a discussion of *possessive adjectives*.)

    The mistake was *mine (ours, yours, hers, his, theirs)*.

    Mine (Ours, Yours, His, Hers, Theirs) was the only part that required revision.

Objective Case

    The editor criticizes *me (us, him, her, one, them, it)*.

2. In the following sentences, supply the missing *personal* and *impersonal* pronouns as shown in the examples:

    The instructor graded the student's paper.

      <u> He </u> graded the student's paper.

    The instructor graded <u> it </u> .

    The governor signed the proclamation.

    <u> She </u> signed <u> it </u> .

1. For very young children, Miss Grant did not stress attention to detail.
   For very young children, _____ did not stress attention to detail.

2. In writing biography and criticism, an author must observe all scholarly traditions.
   In writing biography and criticism, _____ (or _____) must observe all scholarly traditions.

3. Few valid studies of Queen Elizabeth II are concerned with the conditions under which British royalty live.

Few valid studies of Queen Elizabeth II are concerned with the conditions under which _____ live.

4. Mrs. Kaye is responsible for overseeing both sales and marketing.
    _____ is responsible for overseeing both sales and marketing.

5. I decided to give Alice and Bob the portrait they admired so much.
    I decided to give _____ the portrait they admired so much.

6. The agents agreed that John's gift was worth more than expected.
    _____ agreed that _____ was worth more than expected.

7. Your view of London and my view differ widely.
    Your view of London and _____ differ widely.

8. American ballet is particularly interesting since _____ is not confined by tradition.

9. John's view of London and mine differ widely.
    _____ differ widely.

10. Franklin and Eleanor Roosevelt had several children.
    _____ had several children.

11. When submitting manuscripts for publication, the writer must supply two clear copies.
    When submitting manuscripts for publication, _____ (or _____) must supply two clear copies.

12. Whatever preference you may have, the restaurant has a suitable wine.
    Whatever your preference, the restaurant has a wine suitable for _____.

13. Is there no way of forcing the hands of the opposing attorneys?
    Is there no way of forcing _____ hands?

14. Do you know when *Dubliners* was first published?
    Do you know when _____ was first published?

15. It is characteristic of Norma that she agreed to go to the dinner party even though the invitation arrived late.
    It is characteristic of _____ that she agreed to go to the dinner party even though the invitation arrived late.

16. Does this book belong to Stan and Ethel?
    Does this book belong to _____ ?
    Is this book _____ ?

17. I cannot recall whether the poem you refer to is by either Robert or Elizabeth Browning.
    I am certain the poem you refer to is by one of _____.

18. Bill's information was less complete than the information supplied to Louise.
    Bill's information was less complete than the information supplied to _____.

19. No one but Phyllis can do that job properly.
    No one but _____ can do that job properly.

20. Jane was instructed to give the paper to no one but Joe.
    Jane was instructed to give the paper to no one but _____.

21. The Lopez family is going to have its annual reunion.
    _____ are going to have an annual reunion.

22. It is time to give Pooch the medicine the veterinarian prescribed.
    It is time to give Pooch the medicine _____ (or _____) prescribed.

23. Has the cat made a mess again?
    Has _____ made a mess again?

24. Does the painting belong in the neighbors' collection?
     Is the painting one of _____ ?

25. Was the portrait of his first wife?
     Was the portrait _____ ?

Relative Pronouns

Relative pronouns refer to people and objects.
They are used in the three cases:

Subjective	Possessive	Objective
who	whose	whom
that	of that	that
which	of which, whose	which, whom

Who refers to people; *that* to people or objects; *which* to animals, objects, or collective nouns.

The following sentences illustrate the uses of *who*, *that*, and *which* in all their cases:

Subjective Case

A woman *who* wants to succeed in business must dedicate herself to that end.

The boat *that* won the race had an outstanding crew.

Which of the contracts was witnessed by a notary public?

Possessive Case

Whose automobile gave out first?

I have had enough of *that*.

The problem of *which* you spoke has a simple solution.

The board of trustees, *whose* unanimous approval is needed, failed to act in time.

Objective Case

The minor literary figures to *whom* you refer surely merit no further study.

You cannot object to *that*!

The journals to *which* he contributes make no claims about his professional integrity.

American authors to *whom* respect is due include Hemingway, Fitzgerald, and Faulkner.

Whoever, whomever, whichever, and *whatever* are also classified as relative pronouns:

Whoever said Amy would become an outstanding computer programmer must have had a crystal ball.

Give it to *whomever* you decide needs most help.

You have three choices: *whichever* you overlook will bring you nothing but trouble.

Whatever soldiers do, they must be prepared to stand by their actions.

3. In the following sentences, supply the missing *relative pronouns* as shown in these examples:

     __Whoever__ turns in the best essay will receive the award.

     The table __that__ you refinished is standing in the study.

1. This essay, _____ is the worst she has ever written, will surely be judged unworthy of publication.

2. The story _____ I told you must not be repeated.

3. Actresses _____ are good enough for the Broadway stage must surely be good enough for regional theaters.

4. The antiques of _____ you boast may well turn out to be worthless.

5. Plays _____ plots are that obvious cannot hold the interest of any mature audience.

6. Of _____ I have no opinion worth declaring.

7. People in _____ you place great trust are surely special people.

8. The paragraphs to _____ you allude have been lost in the computer printout.

9. The answer to _____ is clearly beyond my limited knowledge.

10. _____ finds the dog will demand a reward for its return.

11. Coats and hats _____ are left in the cloakroom must be claimed by their owners within an hour after the performance.

12. _____ you cite, be certain that your footnote fully credits the source.

13. Horses _____ find their way a great distance from home cannot be thought of as dumb animals.

14. _____ of the two paintings you buy is certainly going to please her.

15. Blue flowers, for _____ I have a special fondness, are not often found in a modern garden.

16. I decided to like _____ she chooses to marry.

17. The house _____ I live in is for sale at any reasonable price.

18. My house, _____ is for sale, sits on a cramped but attractive plot.

19. Houses _____ designs are unconventional may not be readily marketable.

20. Despite her protests, I proceeded to buy the chair _____ she did not want.

21. The partners _____ signed the agreement happily lived to regret doing so.

22. Young men _____ you see in bars are spending their time unwisely.

23. _____ agrees to undertake this project will find that he or she has contracted for a great deal of work.

24. _____ of these minor masterpieces do you prefer?

25. To _____ shall I address the letter of application?

Demonstrative Pronouns

Demonstrative pronouns replace nouns and function in the same manner as nouns in a sentence.

The principal demonstrative pronouns are: *this, that, these,* and *those*. (See *demonstrative adjectives,* page 103.) *This* and *that* are singular. *These* and *those* are plural.

Demonstrative pronouns have no gender, but they do have case.

Subjective	Possessive	Objective
this	of this	this
that	of that	that
these	of these	these
those	of those	those

The following sentences illustrate the uses of the demonstrative pronouns in all their cases:

Subjective Case

This is more than I can possibly eat in one sitting.

That remains my last obstacle to success in college.

These are my only objections to the entire plan.

Those were the bequests that caused so much family wrangling.

Possessive Case

The principal advantages *of this* are economy, beauty, and strength.

Of these, only a few are worthy of full consideration.

Of those, none is worthy of serious comment.

Objective Case

We agreed to give *this* our full attention.

They decided against *that* at least ten years ago.

The harsh weather killed *these* last month.

Choose among *those* and let me know your decisions as soon as possible.

Other demonstrative pronouns commonly encountered are *former, latter, other, such, so, same,* and the ordinal numbers: *first, second, third,* etc.

The following sentences illustrate the use of these demonstrative pronouns:

The *former*, not the *latter,* was the one I intended to bid on.

Such is not the case, despite what you think she said.

He told her *so*.

Now give me the *other*.

Enclosed find payment for *same*.   (Old-fashioned business correspondence usage.)

The *first* was my choice, even though the *fourth* and *sixth* also caught my eye.

4. In the following sentences, supply the missing *demonstrative pronouns* as shown in these examples:

      __This__ suits me better than the previous choice.

      The latter suits me better than the __former__.

1. Indeed, if it were not _____, I surely would have told you by now.
2. I sewed a few of _____ before I went on to a second batch.
3. Let _____ stand as my best effort.
4. He decided to sell me _____ instead of these.
5. Picture _____ hanging in your living room.
6. When you consider famous thoroughbreds of all time, it is doubtful that Secretariat would be the _____ that comes to mind.
7. We ate a little of _____ and a little of _____.
8. We ate a few of _____ and a few of _____.

9. When conditions are _____ that airlines close down flights to our city, we no longer can expect to have full employment.

10. _____ who are willing to stand for office must be willing to debate campaign issues on television.

Interrogative Pronouns

Interrogative pronouns are used in asking questions. The principal interrogative pronouns are *who*, *which*, and *what*. *Whoever* and *whatever* occur less frequently.

Who is used for people. *Which* and *what* are used for things. These pronouns do not have gender.

Subjective	Possessive	Objective
who	whose	whom
which	of which	which
what	of what	what

The following sentences illustrate the uses of interrogative pronouns in all their cases:

Subjective Case

> *Who* stole her collection of compact disks?
> *Which* performs best when the stock market is going down?
> *What* is going to happen to us after she leaves the company?

Possessive Case

> *Whose* did you take?
> *Of which* did you despair first?
> *What* do you think of all day long?

Objective Case

> *Whom* did you take to the senior prom?
> *Which* did you select?
> *What* have you decided to do about the problem we all face?

5. In the following sentences, supply the missing *interrogative pronouns* as shown in these examples:

> ____Who____ has completed the entire English assignment?
> ____What____ can I tell you about her situation?

1. _____ is your favorite classical composer?
2. _____ should we do about all the broken windows?
3. _____ of those birds did my brother Al shoot?
4. _____ were you talking with when I happened to walk by?
5. _____ can you see through the telescope?
6. _____ was playing nine innings of baseball in the rain?
7. _____ do you want me to do for you?

8. _____ is the man Edith praises so much?

9. _____ were you about to do when I interrupted you?

10. _____ do you think of her as a candidate for chief executive?

Reflexive Pronouns

Reflexive pronouns are used in sentences containing verbs whose actions are directed toward the subjects of the verbs. These pronouns are formed by adding *-self* or *-selves*, as appropriate, to the personal pronouns or possessive adjectives *my*, *your*, *him*, *her*, *our*, *them*, *one* and the impersonal pronoun *it*.

The following sentences illustrate the uses of reflexive pronouns:

He almost always cut *himself* while shaving.

You are losing *yourself* in your work.

She discovered *herself* after a period of intense introspection.

Jan usually supported *himself* by teaching karate.

We fail *ourselves* when we fail others.

Ask *yourselves* whether you have done right by your families.

They told *themselves* only what they wanted to hear.

If one only did what was right for *oneself*!

The giraffe found *itself* in trouble after its habitat was thoroughly sprayed with herbicide.

6. In the following sentences, supply the missing *reflexive pronouns* as shown in these examples:

Unfortunately he excused ___himself___ early, leaving us without guidance.

No matter how badly the merchandise was displayed, it seemed to sell ___itself___ .

1. Gary helped _____ to a second large piece of cake.

2. You owe _____ a long vacation far from home.

3. Our wishes _____ are to blame for our most serious faults.

4. Nancy washed _____ in the icy stream.

5. I usually give _____ the benefit of the doubt; doesn't one always give _____ the same advantage?

6. God is said to help those who help _____ .

7. After every meal she ate, the cat washed _____ thoroughly.

8. You should stop fooling _____ about your health.

9. Mr. Saunders made _____ successful through hard work over long years.

10. Pam taught _____ Spanish and French.

11. You men should not blame _____ for what went wrong.

12. I am forcing _____ to lose at least thirty pounds.

13. She will end up hurting _____ if she is not careful.

14. Many a writer has found _____ at loose ends after completing her first novel.

15. The town was ruining _____ by permitting neighboring towns to discharge waste into its sewage system.

Intensive Pronouns

Intensive pronouns are used as appositives (see pages 100–101) to strengthen the subject of a verb.

Intensive pronouns have the same forms as reflexive pronouns: *myself, yourself, himself, herself, ourselves, yourselves, themselves, oneself,* and *itself.*

The following sentences illustrate the uses of the intensive pronouns:

I *myself* can see little use in following a poorly conceived plan.
I can see little use in that action *myself.*
You *yourself* will have to take full responsibility for your budget.
You will have to take full responsibility *yourself.*
Henry *himself* was not at fault in that matter, we have been told.
Henry was not at fault *himself.*
Erica *herself* found little of interest in the new symphony.
Erica found little of interest in the symphony *herself.*
We *ourselves* are content to let the matter drop even though we have been hurt.
We are content *ourselves* to let the matter drop.
You *yourselves* can find the answers if you try hard enough.
You can find the answers *yourselves.*
The French *themselves* are abusing their language.
The French are abusing their language *themselves.*
The magazine *itself* is of little value.
The magazine is of little value *itself.*

7. In the following sentences, supply the missing *intensive pronouns* as shown in these examples:

He could do little   __himself__   to ease the recurrent pain.
Mary   __herself__   found the situation hopelessly ludicrous.

1. We _____ are responsible for most of our own actions.
2. The Jones family _____ was not invited.
3. If he _____ understood the problem, he would find an acceptable answer.
4. One must _____ be alert to people's needs.
5. When I _____ am to blame, I do not hesitate to do what I can to help out.
6. You cannot consider that the two of you have completed the exercise _____.
7. Oscar _____ was a good horseman in most respects.
8. You _____ must find an acceptable solution.
9. Alice was determined to complete the meal _____.
10. Hugh _____ designed and built the house.
11. We concluded that we _____ were entirely free of guilt.
12. Television _____ does little to raise the literacy level in this country.
13. You _____ will have to act as strong leaders or risk losing the election.

14. You will have to show him the way _____.
15. Do you mean that you _____ will do this work without any help?

Reciprocal Pronouns

The *reciprocal pronouns* are *one another* and *each other*. *One another* is generally used when writing of more than two people. Both reciprocal pronouns have *possessive* and *objective* cases.

The following sentences illustrate uses of these pronouns:

> John and Jerry found *each other's* company satisfying.
> All thirty students sought *one another's* assistance.
> He and his wife caught themselves shouting at *each other*.
> He, his wife, and their daughter caught themselves shouting at *one another*.
> Neighbors up and down the road stopped speaking to *one another*.

8. In the following sentences, supply the missing *reciprocal pronouns* as shown in these examples:

> The couple has only __each other__ to blame for mismanaging their budget.
> If the triplets could see __one another__ less frequently, they would be happier.

1. The entire kitchen staff of twelve cooks helped in slicing and buttering _____ bread.
2. The youngest child and his older brothers and sisters all made things as difficult as possible for _____.
3. Gilbert and Sullivan had an intense dislike for_____ during much of their collaboration.
4. He and Mary found_____ company almost unbearable by the time two weeks of summer had passed.
5. We must do for_____ what we would like to have others do for us.
6. They find_____ houses more interesting than their own.
7. Children tend to prefer_____ company to that of most adults.
8. The three wives discovered that there was much they liked about_____.
9. Music and art complement_____ in the lives of many people.
10. All the senior faculty members agreed that there was no practical way they could consult_____ on all problems that had to be resolved.

Indefinite Pronouns

Indefinite pronouns constitute a large number of imprecise words that can function as pronouns. The most frequently used are: *all, another, any, anybody, anyone, anything, both, each one, either, everybody, everyone, everything, few, little, many, more, much, neither, nobody, none, no one, nothing, oneself, other, others, several, some, somebody, someone, something,* and *such*.

The following sentences illustrate some uses of indefinite pronouns:

> *All* we can do is try our best and hope things turn out all right.

This sweater fits *anybody* six or more feet tall.

Each one is reviewed in turn and given a proficiency rating.

I gave him *nothing* for his labors.

If *others* were as concerned as he, there would be no problem.

Someone must be held responsible for this heinous deed.

The crowd was *such* that the police feared a break-in at the gate.

9. In the following sentences, supply the missing *indefinite pronouns* as shown in these examples:

    __Anyone__ portrayed in this manner usually can sue for libel.

    We spoke to ___each one or everyone___ in turn.

    The police suspected that ___something___ had been taken by the intruders.

1. When _____ had left, I began cleaning the auditorium.
2. _____ was able to complete the crossword puzzle, because it was exceptionally difficult.
3. Though many wanted to go aboard, _____ was permitted to do so.
4. Sam said he would buy her _____ she asked for as long as the present would cost less than a hundred dollars.
5. _____ were indicted for perjury, but only two were convicted.
6. The party is open to _____ who wants to contribute to the charity.
7. I gave her most of what I had, but she insisted on having _____ .
8. Unfortunately, there is _____ that can be done.
9. Investigators finally decided that _____ had been taken.
10. When I got through with it, there was _____ left.
11. _____ who works long enough and hard enough is bound to succeed.
12. You can tell me _____ you want, but I probably will not believe you.
13. _____ was discussed, but _____ was done.
14. I have done _____ I can, and now _____ will have to wait and hope.
15. _____ who is completely sane could have committed such a crime.
16. Peter asked _____ he knew, but _____ gave him a straight answer.
17. The weather was _____ that a turbulent flight was inevitable.
18. Only a _____ were able to qualify for the Olympics track events on the first day.
19. People always need _____ to blame their troubles on.
20. _____ was thrown into the water in turn.
21. The smoke bothered almost _____ who was there.
22. _____ were able to pass the examination, but _____ did exceptionally well.
23. Richard told _____ , not even his wife, about the robbery.
24. The books are sitting there, waiting for _____ to read them.
25. Tamara wanted to buy the brown shoes for Sam, but he preferred the _____ .

PRONOUN AGREEMENT

Plural and Singular Antecedents

A pronoun is singular when its antecedent is singular, plural when its antecedent is plural.

Singular and Plural

Any *woman who* is friendly with her neighbors will be well regarded.   (The pronoun *who* is singular, because its antecedent, *woman*, is singular.)

The interesting thing about *John* is that *he* always completes his jokes whether or not *he* has an attentive audience.   (The pronouns *he* and *he* are singular, because their common antecedent, *John*, is singular.)

All three *judges* stated that *they* believed the convict had been accused unjustly.   (The pronoun *they* is plural, because its antecedent, *judges*, is plural.)

Mental health *institutions* care for patients as well as *they* can.   (The pronoun *they* is plural, because its antecedent, *institutions*, is plural.)

10. In the following sentences, supply the *missing pronouns* as shown in these examples:

A file folder must be put back in the place where ___it___ belongs.

Books ___that___ are widely read are frequently stolen.

1. The Mexican government relies heavily on the tourists _____ can attract from the rest of North America.
2. College professors usually say that _____ believe the quality of their students is improving year by year.
3. Radioactive wastes can be a threat to the lives of the residents of a town if _____ do not take steps to safeguard their water supply.
4. After Hazel and Harry had finished their work, _____ went to the movies.
5. The New York Yankees, _____ flourished during the era of Babe Ruth, have found _____ frequently longing for his return.
6. _____ of the three virtuoso violinists is best known by concertgoers?
7. After an electrical storm leaves an area, _____ either dissipates or goes on to do its mischief in another area.
8. English teachers continue to make the same mistakes in the classroom _____ have always made.
9. General Motors, _____ of the largest enterprises in the world, is always conscious of the public image it projects.
10. The policeman said that _____ had caught all three burglars as _____ were leaving the store.
11. Many experts deny the authenticity of that Vermeer, claiming that _____ lacks the quality of light _____ associate with the master.
12. Although _____ do not often admit their debt, many Americans would be lost if _____ could not turn to their freezers and microwave ovens a half hour before starting dinner.
13. A man _____ is true to his own conscience may find _____ in trouble with the authorities.

14. Howard Carter, _____ studied in Egypt in 1922, discovered the tomb of Tutankhamen, the famous Egyptian king _____ died when _____ was only eighteen.

15. My neighbor is good at training her own two horses, but not _____ that _____ boards.

16. In the middle of the examination, I broke my pencil and was not allowed to sharpen _____ .

17. Roger left on a trip to Peru without remembering to carry the Spanish dictionary _____ needed so badly.

18. Of all the plays of Shakespeare, *King Lear* is the one I like best, although the other tragedies surpass _____ as far as my wife is concerned.

19. _____ of Dora's cats is gentler, the brown or the gray?

20. This book, _____ I found in a secondhand bookstore, is proving _____ valuable.

21. Graham Greene is much admired for his early novels, but many say that _____ like all the work _____ published.

22. Fujiyama is a famous tourist attraction, but many tourists complain that on most days _____ are not able to see _____ .

23. Anne Frank recorded her deepest fears and hopes in a diary _____ kept during the tragic events of World War II, but never saw _____ published.

24. After fighting the fish for hours, the fisherman found that _____ could not bring _____ in.

25. When Joe DiMaggio was in his prime, _____ was the hero of all young boys, _____ dreamed of seeing _____ play one day.

Antecedents Joined by *And, Or,* or *Nor*

Plural

A pronoun is plural when its antecedent is two or more words joined by *and*.

> *Richard and Jeffrey* are completing undergraduate degrees *they* hope to put to use.
> *Boys and girls* are finding *themselves* increasingly disenchanted with school.

Singular

A pronoun is singular when its antecedent is two or more singular words joined by *or* or *nor*.

> I don't know whether *Joan or Edna* made *herself* clear in the argument.
> Neither *Sinclair Lewis nor Thomas Wolfe* has yet received the final critical judgment *he* deserves.

When a singular antecedent and a plural antecedent are joined by *or* or *nor*, the pronoun agrees in number with the antecedent that is closer.

> Either Barbara or the *twins* will have to do what *they* can.
> Neither the salesmen nor the *manager* learned that *he* was at fault.
> Neither the manager nor the *salesmen* learned that *they* were at fault.

If use of this rule risks ambiguity, the sentence must be recast.

11. In the following sentences supply the *missing pronouns* as shown in these examples:

> A male sibling and his sisters sometimes go through life without knowing what ___they___ really believe.
>
> I cannot understand why the brothers believe ___they___ will work together harmoniously.
>
> If a hotel or motel opens its doors next year, ___it___ will be operating profitably within two years.

1. Neither Idaho nor Montana can boast of the severe winter weather _____ receives.
2. The mountains and beaches are crowded by tourists every year even though _____ are becoming increasingly inaccessible.
3. My parents raise cows and sheep even though _____ are not profitable.
4. We have been given our paychecks, but neither Carole nor Susan has received _____ yet.
5. Either the brothers or the sister will have to pay her debt before the credit manager will give _____ additional credit.
6. Either the sister or the brothers will have to pay their debt before the credit manager will give _____ additional credit.
7. Neither the union members nor their leaders showed any interest in a quick settlement of the dispute between _____.
8. Either the union president or the members will have to show interest in a quick settlement if _____ are to have labor peace.
9. The librarians and the library board are meeting tonight to adopt the budget we offered _____ for next year.
10. Neither Ted nor his brothers found _____ were entirely happy when the family attorney read their father's will aloud.

Collective Nouns

If an antecedent is a collective noun treated as singular, the pronoun affected by it is singular.

> The committee *is* meeting next week to reach the decision *it* wants.
>
> The board of trustees *has decided* to name as chairperson the candidate *it* first met.

If an antecedent is a collective noun treated as plural, the pronoun is plural.

> The committee *are* meeting next week to reach the decision *they* want.
>
> The board of trustees *have* decided to reverse the decision *they* made.

Collective nouns must be treated consistently within a given unit of writing. They must never be treated as both singular and plural.

12. In the following sentences, supply the *missing pronouns* as shown in these examples:

> The board of directors has not met since ___it___ recessed in January.
>
> The board of directors have been in constant consultation, because ___they___ anticipate a growing fiscal problem.

1. The debating team is having its best season since _____ was organized.
2. The steering committee are meeting to declare that _____ intend to strike.
3. No organization has a future if its members are not willing to support _____.
4. I would be willing to be a member of a group that stands up for the positions _____ believes in.
5. The contents of the box are stamped on the top, but _____ can scarcely be read without a magnifying glass.
6. Across the street live a couple who soon will announce that _____ are grandparents.
7. A dozen is too much for a small meal and too little for a large one, but _____ might be just right for a bedtime snack.
8. My offspring are going to be permitted to go to the theater by _____.
9. The company has sponsored a picnic every summer since _____ started in business.
10. A jury usually is not unanimous in its judgment unless one attorney or the other is extremely skillful in arguing before _____.

Singular Pronouns as Antecedents

A singular pronoun is used with any of the following pronouns as antecedent: *one, anyone, anybody, someone, somebody, everyone, everybody, each, kind, sort, either, neither, no one, nobody.*

> *Everyone* who thinks realistically that *he* or *she* can write professionally needs an agent.   (*Everyone* is the antecedent of *he* or *she*.)
> *Each* of the actors in the audition recited the lines *he* knew best.
> The right *sort* of book will inevitably find a market for *itself*.

13.   In the following sentences, supply the *missing pronouns* as shown in the examples:

> Neither Manuel nor Juan was willing to say that ___he___ knew the answers.
> Anyone who works hard will receive the reward ___he or she___ deserves.

1. I would like to locate somebody _____ does house painting.
2. Somebody has to do his (her) work better than _____ has been doing it, or somebody will find _____ out of a job.
3. No one can do more than _____ has done to help people less fortunate.
4. He recommended the sort of program that usually commends _____ to the uninformed viewer.
5. Anybody who finds _____ in conflict with the law is well advised to find _____ a lawyer.
6. Mary found *For Whom the Bell Tolls* the sort of book that works its way deep into the conscience of any sensitive person who reads _____.
7. One of the eggs was still sticking to the pan, asssserting that _____ had a right to remain uneaten.
8. Either of the girls considers _____ fortunate when she has enough to eat.

9. Students were asked to share their dorm rooms, but nobody wanted to be the first to offer
   _____.

10. A woman who asserts _____ is the kind of woman needed for an executive
    position.

11. He found that each of the defects became immediately apparent once _____ was
    pointed out.

12. The Dean of Women claimed that no one in the women's dormitory was interested in
    stepping forward to declare _____ available for a leadership job.

13. Neither of the organizations desired to review the entire spectrum of policies _____
    stood for.

14. Everybody in the extended community was going to assert _____.

15. One of the fellows was denied permission to complete the project by _____.

16. Any sort of food is acceptable as long as _____ is palatable.

17. Anyone who wants to use my razor can do so if _____ is willing to clean it
    afterwards.

18. Either was acceptable, provided that _____ met the full test of credibility.

19. Everybody will be allowed to join as long as _____ has the initiation fee.

20. She declared that no one had established full claim to ownership, because no one had filed
    the papers _____ was obliged to supply.

PRONOUNS IN THE SUBJECTIVE CASE

A pronoun used as the subject of a verb is in the *subjective case*.

She was one of the brightest pupils in the school.
I know that most people want to marry.
The people *who* were willing to wait in line found that *they* were able to purchase tickets
at a reduced rate.
The concert that *he* attended was rewarding.

14. In the following sentences supply the *missing pronouns* as shown in these examples:

By the time their dinner was over,   we or you or they   were exhausted.
Ruth found that ___she___ was unable to complete her work.

1. _____ is the most beautiful flower in the entire greenhouse.

2. _____ among you is willing to take over the job I am leaving?

3. I told her that _____ was the most talented artist in the class.

4. The roles _____ played made John Barrymore sought after by all theatrical
   producers.

5. Pablo Casals was able to perform in concert even when _____ was in his
   nineties.

6. Owners of little dogs must see to it that _____ always have enough to eat and
   drink.

7. Persian melons are not always as succulent as _____ appear to be.

8. *The Tempest* appeals to me more and more each time _____ see it.

9. A telephone company employee _____ helps customers in times of emergency is eligible for a special award.

10. A United States Senator _____ is present on the floor of the Senate during debate is as rare as _____ is valuable to the community _____ serves.

PRONOUNS IN THE OBJECTIVE CASE

A pronoun used as the object or indirect object of a verb is in the *objective case*.

Veterinarians inspect *them* each year.

Lawyers can be counted on to give *us* competent interpretations of the penal code.

15. In the following sentences, supply the *missing pronouns* as shown in these examples:

The firm dismissed _him or her or them or us or you or me_ for no apparent reason.

The outfielder tossed _her_ the ball, because she asked for it.

1. Although Mrs. Gilbert testified that I had misled her, I insist that I told _____ the entire truth before asking _____ to sign my petition.

2. The boy to _____ I gave the book is no longer a member of the group.

3. _____ shall we invite to the office party?

4. They decided to give _____ trouble, because I would not be a party to their conniving.

5. Television can distract _____ from our legitimate work.

6. Going to chamber music recitals gave _____ much pleasure in their old age.

7. Would you find it wrong of _____ to offer _____ my hand when you are leaving a bus?

8. His mother slapped _____ as hard as she could when she realized that he had told lies.

9. _____ must we send the last five copies to?

10. Is there any way we can find of helping _____ anonymously when she needs help?

Pronouns as Objects of Verbals

A pronoun used as the object or indirect object of a verbal is in the *objective case*.

Having surveyed *it*, the general decided that the river could not be forded.   (*it* direct object of past participle *having surveyed*.)

While questioning *me*, the accountant found many more legitimate tax deductions.   (*me* direct object of present participle *questioning*.)

To give *him* all the credit he deserves, I will grant that he tried hard.   (*him* indirect object of infinitive *to give*.)

Fighting *her* proved more difficult than I expected.   (*her* direct object of gerund *fighting*.)

16. In the following sentences, supply the *missing pronouns* as shown in the examples:

> Constantly quizzing ___them___ is not going to make your students happier.
> We wanted to distract ___her___ as much as possible, so she would spend her last days contentedly.

1. The staff insists that everything possible be done for students to give _____ the opportunity they need.
2. Troublemakers are not going to be changed by restricting _____ to a few areas.
3. Having invited _____, we must do all we can to treat our guests well.
4. Memorizing a role is not as difficult as performing _____.
5. After capturing enemy soldiers, we must treat _____ humanely.
6. To give _____ his due, Juan has always been faithful to the people.
7. While we have been able to identify child abuse, we are having difficulty in eradicating _____.
8. To prepare for examinations is only half the job; we also have the responsibility to pass _____.
9. Elizabeth found herself facing all her problems honestly, but failing in her efforts to solve _____.
10. Her guest had stayed so late that my sister decided to invite _____ to have some breakfast.

Pronouns as Objects of Prepositions

A pronoun used as the object of a preposition is in the *objective case*.

> We spoke to *her* as forcefully as possible.
> The librarian promptly gave the manuscript to *him*.
> To *whom* did you deliver the bouquet?

17. In the following sentences supply the *missing pronouns* as shown in these examples:

> Susan's mother often asked for ___her or him or me or us or them or you___.
> The cat trailed after ___me___ all day long, even though I tried to get away from ___it___.

1. Annie does not care for a moment that people are talking about _____.
2. Try as hard as we can, we cannot choose among _____.
3. The subject was clearly beyond _____, so I decided to end my presentation.
4. As Dick looked out upon the city, he felt that all he had to do was reach out and grasp what lay before _____.
5. Within _____ was beautiful music waiting to be released by the young composer.
6. His mother proved obdurate: he had received the last dollar he would ever get from _____.
7. By _____ was this obscene letter written?
8. Inside _____ still was the fear he had known for so long.

9. Among _____ are two or three lucky individuals who will win substantial amounts; the rest will insist their fees had been taken from _____ without a chance of winning.

10. After learning that Rebecca had paid for the book, we returned the money to _____.

PRONOUNS IN THE POSSESSIVE CASE

A pronoun indicating possession is in the *possessive case*.

> *Yours* is the last one I will accept.
>
> Jon made full restitution because the book he destroyed proved to be *mine*.
>
> *Whose* will you be carrying?

18. In the following sentences supply the *missing pronouns* as shown in the examples:

> We found ___his or hers___ the best of the entries.
>
> ___Theirs___ had been damaged, but not ___mine___.

1. Our book had been left unopened all those years, so _____ was used.
2. We took everything they made, because _____ were the least expensive and most reliable tables available.
3. Several artists entered paintings in the competition. _____ did you choose?
4. Harry told us _____ was best because we had completely thought through the problem.
5. Ellen phrased _____ so carefully and appropriately that mine was totally ignored by all the judges on the committee.
6. All things considered, Amy prefers to market _____ because she admires the work we do.
7. Jon and Rory enjoy their new home more than we can possibly enjoy _____.
8. Reading is valuable for their children as well as for _____.
9. If you will do without yours, I will do without _____.
10. When the big contributor announces her generous gift, we will announce _____.

PRONOUNS AS APPOSITIVES

A pronoun used as an appositive—a word or phrase that explains or identifies a word or phrase nearby—is in the same case as the word with which it is in apposition.

Subjective

> We, Linda and *I*, will underwrite the cost of Sam's education.   (*I* is in the subjective case because it is in apposition with *We*, the subject of the verb *will underwrite*.)

Objective

> All the damage incurred in the accident was caused by us, Mickey and *me*.   (*Me* is in the objective case because it is in apposition with *us*, the object of a preposition.)

Possessive

> She asked whose bicycle had been broken, Margaret's or *mine*.   (*Mine* is in the possessive case because it is in apposition with *whose*, which is a possessive adjective.)

19.   In the following sentences, supply the *missing pronouns* as shown in these examples:

> We, John and ___I___ , can do all the work.
>
> She found us, Carole and ___me___ , in the midst of preparing dinner for eight people.
>
> I asked him whose class met first, ___his___ or mine?

1. The judge was stern to both of us, the claimant's attorney and _____ .

2. Both of us, the district attorney and _____ , were called before the judge.

3. I do not know whose interests are being considered, but I believe we should take care of our own, yours and _____ , before we worry about a stranger's.

4. The old man's will referred to the two of them, Robert and _____ , as "good sons and worthy."

5. The two of us, Jenny and _____ , were invited to the same inaugural ball.

6. Walsh likely will invite neither of us, Emma nor _____ .

7. We both have an interest in the matter, and I wonder whose understanding is closer to the truth, yours or _____ .

8. Both our families, his and _____ , are uncomfortable at the thought of another dismal reunion.

9. Last year's election found us, my wife and _____ , ill prepared to vote with any degree of enthusiasm.

10. We could find no valid solutions for our joint problems, she in regard to financial matters and _____ in regard to social relationships.

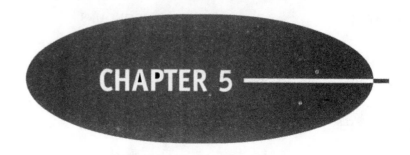

CHAPTER 5

Adjectives

Adjectives modify nouns and pronouns:

A *happy* **man** faces each day optimistically.   (The adjective *happy* modifies *man*, a noun.)

The *first* **one** to finish receives a prize.   (The adjective *first* modifies *one*, a pronoun.)

Adjectives may also be used to complete a copulative verb:

Alice *is sad*, because her son pays her little attention.   (The adjective *sad* completes the copulative verb *is*. Such an adjective is called a *predicate adjective*.)

1. Underline the *adjectives* in the following sentences as shown in these examples:

<u>Green</u> leaves are <u>one sure</u> sign of spring.

<u>Weak</u> men feel <u>strong</u> when they achieve success.

   1. Ten apples are enough for two large pies.

   2. Oaken buckets were used by early settlers.

   3. The only one I saw was a little child.

   4. Hard cheese can be eaten with great delight.

   5. An orange jacket is advisable on a ski slope.

TYPES OF ADJECTIVES

There are three types of adjectives: *descriptive*, *limiting*, and *proper*.

Descriptive adjectives name a quality or condition of the element modified: a *perfect* marriage, a *red* dress, an *honest* attorney, *running* water, a *broken* axle.

Limiting adjectives identify or enumerate the element modified: *that* table, *present* company, *many* illnesses, *his* love, *seven* days, *fifth* stanza.

Proper adjectives are descriptive adjectives that are derived from proper names: *Indian* customs, *French* perfume, *Austrian* cuisine, *Chinese* checkers, *African* violets.

2. In the following sentences, classify the adjectives as *descriptive*, *limiting*, or *proper* as shown in these examples:

> The lecturer spent *his* time on *French* culture, not history.
>
> *his*, limiting; *French*, proper
>
> *Beautiful* volumes have appeared in *that* series.
>
> *Beautiful*, descriptive; *that*, limiting

1. *Improper* accounting almost ruined *her catering* business.

2. *Careful* analysis uncovered *several* flaws in *his experimental* data.

3. *Mexican* food is not favored by *his* parents.

4. *Poor* Willy lost *his Irish* setter.

5. *One* dish does not a *perfect* meal make.

Limiting Adjectives

Limiting adjectives are classified according to their functions as *demonstrative*, *indefinite*, *interrogative*, *numerical*, *possessive*, or *relative*.

A *demonstrative* adjective indicates or specifies the noun or pronoun it modifies: *this* one, *that* one, *these* men, *those* women.

An *indefinite* adjective indicates more broadly the noun or pronoun it modifies: *all* people, *any* person, *each* one, *most* people, *many* pennies, *no* book, *some* support, *several* others. There are many other indefinite adjectives.

An *interrogative* adjective asks a question as it modifies a noun or pronoun: *Whose* hat is missing? *What* time is it? *Which* one will you take?

A *numerical* adjective specifies a number as it modifies a noun or pronoun. Numerical adjectives may be either cardinal or ordinal. *Cardinal*: *six* robins, *twenty-four* ounces. *Ordinal*: *third* horse, *first* violin, *thirty-sixth* President of the United States.

A *possessive* adjective denotes ownership as it modifies a noun or pronoun: *my* mistake, *one's* tennis serve, *his* elbow, *her* prerogative, *its* aroma, *our* company, *their* pride.

A *relative* adjective introduces a subordinate clause that modifies a noun or pronoun. *Whose* is the only relative adjective. Its function is illustrated in the following sentence:

> The lad *whose* mother died has left school. (The subordinatae clause *whose mother died* modifies *lad*. The clause is introduced by the relative adjective *whose*, which is part of the modifier.)

3. In the following sentences, identify the *italicized limiting adjectives* as *demonstrative*, *indefinite*, *interrogative*, *numerical*, *possessive*, or *relative* as shown in these examples:

> *Which* side are you on?
>
> interrogative

My *first* bad mistake was followed by *many* others.
  first, numerical; *many*, indefinite

1. *His* ignorance was matched by *his* stupidity.

2. *Eleven* players are needed if we are to have a good game.

3. She asked advice of *her* mother before cooking breakfast for *her* sisters.

4. *That* shirt goes well with *both my* suits.

5. *What* nonsense are you telling me?

6. Police officers *whose* only duties are clerical receive the same pay that *all* patrol officers receive.

7. *Each* sentence he spoke revealed *his* disappointment.

8. *No* decent person would ever hold such opinions.

9. Parents *whose* children play baseball have been known to carry on like maniacs.

10. *Their* turn is next in the examining room.

11. *His* shoelaces were untied once again.

12. *Which* channel did she waste *her* time on last night?

13. The *first* point to remember is that *her* role is worthy of recognition.

14. *That* boy will be the *only* one in *your* class.

15. *Any* student who uses material without proper attribution is guilty of plagiarism.

Predicate Adjectives

Predicate adjectives complete copulative, or linking, verbs: *act, be, become, feel, prove, seem*, etc.

Copulative verbs are also completed by *predicate nouns*. Together, predicate adjectives and predicate nouns are referred to as *predicate complements*. (See page 22.)

The following sentences illustrate both types of predicate complements:

She acts *sick* whenever Monday arrives.   (The copulative verb *acts* has as its complement *sick*; *sick* is an adjective, so *sick* is a predicate adjective.)

Anne is a *radiologist*.   (Because *radiologist* is a noun, *radiologist* is a *predicate noun*.)

Harry is *happy*.   (Because *happy* is an adjective, *happy* is a *predicate adjective*.)

4. In the following sentences, underline the *predicate adjectives* as shown in these examples:

> He will act <u>happier</u> as time goes by.
> Dick became an editor.   (none)

    1. This print looks fine to me.
    2. Jane's story was excellent.
    3. Henry's first novel was exciting.
    4. She felt bad.
    5. I feel better this morning.
    6. Her hair appeared radiant.
    7. Bob's nose has become larger.
    8. This is the best novel I own.
    9. Jenny appears disconsolate.
    10. Pogo acts sad when Ray leaves for work.

POSITION OF ADJECTIVES

Except for predicate adjectives, adjectives are usually placed next to the nouns or pronouns they modify, and the most common position of all is immediately before the element modified:

> *beautiful* shoes, *happy* child, *old* woman   (descriptive adjectives)
> *this* book, *many* poems, *six* months   (limiting adjectives)
> *Greek* grammar, *Italian* cooking, *Russian* music   (proper adjectives)

In some constructions, adjectives can also be placed immediately after the element modified:

> a poem *short* and *beautiful*   (The writer has chosen this construction for its pleasing rhythm.)
> attorney *general*, court-*martial*   (These terms were expressed this way in French and are accepted as English expressions.)
> a tale so *sad* that all who heard it cried   (Because the adjective *sad* is itself modified by the clause that follows, its normal position is changed.)

Except in rare constructions, predicate adjectives follow the verbs they complete:

> Jack looked *doubtful*.
> Barbara seemed *angry*.
> John felt *hopeless*.
> *Innocent* was the Child.   (This type of construction is reserved for special stylistic effect.)

5. Insert adjectives in appropriate positions in the following sentences as shown in these examples:

> *oldest*   The brother played the role of father to the five children.
>   <u>oldest brother</u>

> *happy*   Many patients in mental hospitals appear despite their troubles.
>   <u>appear happy</u>

1. *fresh*   We hoped that trout would satisfy his hunger.
    _____

2. *rare*   Books were his sole source of satisfaction.
    _____

3. *Italian*   The Metropolitan no longer relies solely on opera.
    _____

4. *ripe*   The pear was treat enough for the child.
    _____

5. *exciting*   Some novels are so that I cannot put them down.
    _____

COMPARISON OF ADJECTIVES

Adjectives have three comparative forms: *absolute*, *comparative*, and *superlative* to indicate greater or lesser degrees of the quality described:

Absolute	Comparative	Superlative
sweet	sweeter	sweetest
fine	finer	finest
intelligent	more intelligent	most intelligent
beautiful	more beautiful	most beautiful

The comparative form of the great majority of adjectives can be achieved in two ways: by adding *-er* to the absolute or by adding the adverb *more*. Similarly, the superlative can be achieved in two ways: by adding *-est* to the absolute or by adding the adverb *most*. Some adjectives change forms radically to express comparison: *good, better, best; bad, worse, worst*.

The comparative form is used when discussing two items or individuals, the superlative form when discussing three or more:

> Of the two sisters, Nola is the *more intelligent*.
> Of the fifty states, Vermont is the *most beautiful*.
> She is a *better* student than her brother.
> She was the *best* student I had ever known.

The comparative is also used when comparing a single item or individual with a class of items or individuals:

> She was a *better* swimmer than any of the men in her school.
> That mountain is *taller* by far than any of the mountains in our state.

6. Supply the proper comparative or superlative forms of the adjectives in the following sentences, as shown in these examples:

> Dorothy was a (good) cook than her sister.   __better__
> Julian was the (good) copywriter in New York City.   __best__

1. Broccoli usually tastes (good) when cooked in oil than in butter.   _____
2. I believe my social security checks will be (small) than yours.   _____

3. The (young) student in the class may not always be the most precocious. _____
4. I found his style (suitable) to fiction than to journalism. _____
5. Hawaii formerly had the (broad) ethnic mixture of any state. _____
6. Richard finds his new assistant (competent) than he expected. _____
7. A fine painting is worth more aesthetically than the (good) photograph money can buy. _____
8. Of all the paintings by Renoir in the Metropolitan Museum of Art, the (good) one is practically ignored by the public. _____
9. I believe the coastline of California is (long) than that of any other state in the country. _____
10. I believe California has the (long) coastline in the country. _____

ADJECTIVE PHRASES

An adjective phrase is a phrase used to modify nouns or pronouns. Adjective phrases are formed by combining a preposition with a noun or pronoun and its modifiers:

> The chair *in the living room* needs to be repaired. (The phrase *in the living room* modifies the noun *chair*. The preposition *in* has *room* as its object. *Room* is modified by *the living*.)
> The one *in the rear* is my choice. (*in the rear* modifies the pronoun *one*.)

The most common prepositions are *at, between, by, for, from, in, of, on, through, to,* and *with*.

Adjective phrases must be kept near the word or words they modify in order to achieve clarity. They usually are placed immediately after the words they modify.

7. In the following sentences, underline the *adjective phrases* as shown in these examples:

> The girl <u>with the flaxen hair</u> is my daughter.
> The light <u>at the end of the tunnel</u> is dim.

1. Communication between you and me is no longer satisfactory.
2. Assistance for indigent persons is a social obligation.
3. Hats are not worn as often as milliners with failing businesses would like.
4. The applicants with little hope are complaining loudly.
5. Those with substantial fortunes are happiest about the stock market.
6. Gardens between houses are well tended in my town.
7. The best of the Impressionist paintings have never been shown in the United States.
8. The view through my window is as lively as ever.
9. The telephone lines to Europe are seldom out.
10. He found that the lesion on his right lung was healing rapidly.

ADJECTIVE CLAUSES

An adjective clause is a clause used to modify nouns or pronouns. Like all clauses, adjective clauses usually consist of subject, verb, modifiers, and object if appropriate.

Consider the following sentences:

Every change *that is made between now and opening night* will cause difficulty for the actors.   (The adjective clause *that is made between now and opening night* modifies the noun *change*.)

Anyone *who insists on getting his due* must be persistent.   (The adjective clause *who insists on getting his due* modifies the pronoun *anyone*.)

Adjective clauses are often introduced by relative pronouns—*that, which, who*, etc.—as shown in the preceding examples. Many times the relative pronouns are omitted:

The woman *I have shared my life with all these years* is standing beside me now.

Gardens *he has tended* have never won horticultural prizes.

Adjective clauses must be kept close to the word or words they modify in order to achieve clarity. They usually are placed immediately after the words they modify.

8.   In the following sentences, underline the *adjective clauses* as shown in these examples:

The evidence <u>they left behind</u> was enough to incriminate them.

Instructors <u>who wish to teach well</u> must prepare their lectures carefully.

1. They found the papers that had been missing for many years.
2. These animals, which are indigenous to Africa, will not survive in cold climates.
3. Engineers, who are skillful in interpreting scientific data, are not usually capable of conducting original research.
4. Children who find their immediate desires blocked may react by throwing temper tantrums.
5. Wines of quality that have been stored properly will retain their bouquet for years.
6. Books I have treasured since childhood still intrigue me today.
7. He found a wounded animal that had managed to survive without care.
8. The meal he plans to cook today will be rich in flavor.
9. The tree she felled with her little hatchet is surprisingly large.
10. Anyone who has found himself unable to find a job will sympathize with those who are habitually unemployed.

Restrictive and Nonrestrictive Adjective Clauses

A restrictive adjective clause is one that is essential in defining or limiting a noun or pronoun:

The girl *I admire most* is one who stands up for her rights.   (*I admire most* identifies *girl*, limiting the general noun *girl* to one particular girl.)

A nonrestrictive adjective clause is one that is not essential in defining or limiting a noun or pronoun:

This one, *which I have nurtured for many years*, is not a particularly attractive shrub.   (The pronoun *one* is modified by *which I have nurtured for many years*, but the modifier does not identify *one* in a way that makes *one* distinctive. The modifier that does make *one* distinctive is *This*. The nonrestrictive modifier *which I have nurtured for many years* gives us useful, but not essential, information.)

Nonrestrictive modifiers are set off by punctuation, while restrictive modifiers are not. Consider the following sentences:

The word processor *I bought* often breaks down.   (The restrictive modifier *I bought* is not set off by commas and cannot be omitted from the sentence without changing its meaning in a critical way. *I bought* is needed to identify the word processor.)

My word processor, *which I paid $1500 for years ago*, is still working well.   (The modifying clause *which I paid $1500 for years ago* is nonrestrictive. It can be omitted without changing meaning.)

9. In the following sentences, underscore the *adjective clauses*, identify them as *restrictive* or *nonrestrictive*, and supply any *punctuation* needed, as shown in these examples:

> I gave the money to the one who needed it most.   restrictive
> Apple trees, which are both beautiful and productive, do not live forever. nonrestrictive

1. He learned little from the research papers he wrote in his English courses. _____
2. Ships of Panamanian registry that were active in the period between the two world wars are still seen today. _____
3. Curries that have been left unrefrigerated lose their attractive taste rapidly. _____
4. Pets that have served their masters well are often allowed to die in pain. _____
5. She has a smile that conveys gratitude but little warmth. _____
6. The book I consult most often is the dictionary. _____
7. African-Americans who have made many important cultural contributions to our country are often reviled by the ignorant. _____
8. Swiss cheese which has a distinctive texture and appearance is sold throughout the world. _____
9. More maple syrup is processed in New York State than in Vermont which calls itself the world leader in maple syrup production. _____
10. The multinational corporation which is a relatively new phenomenon has become a powerful force in international politics as well as economics. _____

That and *Which* with Adjective Clauses

It is customary to use *that* to introduce restrictive adjective clauses; *which* to introduce nonrestrictive adjective clauses. When the relative pronoun can be omitted before an adjective clause, the clause is restrictive. Consider the following sentences:

The book *that I bought yesterday* has been stolen.   (The adjective clause *that I bought yesterday* is restrictive, since it cannot be omitted without making *book* unidentifiable. As a restrictive clause, it is introduced by *that*. No commas are used to set off the clause. Because the clause is restrictive, the relative pronoun *that* can be omitted: The book *I bought yesterday* has been stolen.)

Cabell's first book, *which was one of my favorites*, is no longer in print.   (The adjective clause *which was one of my favorites* is nonrestrictive. For this reason it is introduced by *which* and is set off by commas. The relative pronoun *which* cannot be omitted.)

10. Insert *that* or *which* in the following sentences and supply needed *punctuation*, as shown in these examples:

> Clothing *that* we buy with our own money fits well.
>
> This coat, *which* I bought in a pawn shop, fits better than I expected.

1. The pipe I left behind was one of the best I ever owned.
2. My last dollar I wanted to spend on food was supposed to keep me alive until payday.
3. Two quarts of milk cost much less than a pound of meat have more food value as far as I am concerned.
4. Yesterday's newspaper was left on my doorstep belongs to my neighbor.
5. The message the fiery minister conveys is not to be ignored.

NOUNS USED AS ADJECTIVES

Nouns often function as adjectives: the *Carter* years, the *Nixon* White House, the *Clinton* administration, the *barber* shop, the *tailor* shop, the *toy* store, the *stationery* store, *college* life, *organization* man, *street* smarts.

11. In the following sentences, underline the *nouns* used as *adjectives* as shown in these examples:

> Such a woman was once known as a <u>grass</u> widow.
>
> Give me the <u>bachelor</u> life.

1. The senator could do with a little book learning.
2. Farmer cheese is hard to find in supermarkets.
3. After he left the police force, he became a store detective.
4. Phonograph records are no longer sold in most music stores.
5. Progressive furniture manufacturers employ industrial designers.

Adjectives Used as Nouns

Just as nouns can be used as adjectives, many adjectives can be used as nouns: the *high* and *mighty*, *The Best and the Brightest*, *The Naked and the Dead*, *The Just and the Unjust*, the *rich*, the *poor*, the *destitute*.

12. In the following sentences, underline the *adjectives* used as *nouns*, as shown in these examples:

> The <u>lame</u> and the <u>halt</u> gathered before her.
>
> He was expert in treating the <u>old</u> as well as the <u>young.</u>

1. The proud will one day have to learn humility.
2. Our country has always been known for its sympathy for the poor.
3. The race is not always to the swift.
4. The wealthy are turned away along with the indigent.
5. Who is there among us who does not respect the learned?

PARTICIPLES AS ADJECTIVES

Present and past participles are often used as adjectives: *used* cars, *growing* pains, *worn* tires, *leaning* tower. Like other adjectives, present and past participles may themselves be modified by adverbs and prepositional phrases.

Consider the following sentences:

Watching carefully, he saw everything the men did. (The present participle *watching* modifies the pronoun *he* and is itself modified by the adverb *carefully*.)

The brisket, *barbecuing* slowly, gave off tantalizing aromas. (The present participle *barbecuing* modifies the noun *brisket* and is itself modified by the adverb *slowly*.)

Marilyn Monroe, *adored* by many, died prematurely. (The past participle *adored* modifies *Marilyn Monroe* and is itself modified by the prepositonal phrase *by many*.)

Participles used as adjectives may also take an object.

Watching her carefully, he quickly learned the secret of the tennis backhand. (The participle *watching* modifies *he* and has as its object *her*. It is also modified, of course, by *carefully*.)

The detective, alertly *pursuing* every clue, finally decided that the butler had not committed the crime. (The participle *pursuing* modifies *detective* and has as its object *clue*. The participle *pursuing* is modified by the adverb *alertly*.)

13. In the following sentences, underline the *participles* used as *adjectives*, as shown in these examples:

    Running water is often fit for drinking by animals, but not by human beings.

    Changing quickly to his official uniform, the police officer began to pursue the suspect.

    1. Some cities actually defaulted on their bonds, sold as safe investments.
    2. Undeterred by the teacher's warnings, the class continued to delay work on the final project.
    3. Struggling against the undertow, Alice managed to reach shore.
    4. Sprinkled lightly on a salad, rosemary can bring out the flavor of the most common garden lettuce.
    5. Police officers, victimized by crime themselves, often harbor fear and hostility toward ordinary citizens.
    6. Many of my books, unopened on my library shelves, ought to be given to hospitals or to the Salvation Army.
    7. She finally abandoned the project, finding it dull and unrewarding.
    8. Harassed and dispirited, Lucy decided to give up the oboe.

9. Gasping for breath, the marathon runners completed the long race.

10. Once achieved, a college education can be regarded with some affection.

Dangling Participles

When a participle functions as an adjective, care must be taken to make sure the reader can easily identify the noun or pronoun the participle modifies. When the reader is left uncertain of what is being modified, the writer's mistake is referred to as a *dangling participle*.

Consider the following sentences:

Dangling

Cooked rare, I could not chew the steak.   (Obviously *I* was not *cooked rare*. The *steak* was. But *rare* is too close to *I*.)

Correct

I could not chew the steak because it was cooked rare.

Dangling

While watching closely, my leather handbag was stolen.   (Obviously *my handbag* was not *watching* anything. Who was *watching*? *I* was watching. But *I* is not in the sentence.)

Correct

While I was watching closely, my leather handbag was stolen.

Dangling

Strolling blissfully down the garden path, *I* saw a scorpion.   (Who was *strolling*? Assuming that *I* was, the sentence can be recast one way. Assuming that the scorpion was, the sentence can be recast another way.)

Correct

While I was strolling blissfully down the garden path, I saw a scorpion.

While walking today, I saw a scorpion blissfully strolling down the garden path.

Dangling participles are corrected, therefore, by (1) rearranging the sentence to bring the participle closer to the nouns or pronouns being modified, (2) inserting the missing words to be modified, or (3) rewriting the sentence completely.

14. Where necessary, correct the following sentences as shown in these examples:

While thinking of the approaching examinations, my class came to an abrupt end.
  While I was thinking of the approaching examinations, my class came to an abrupt end.

Completely taken by surprise, she offered no resistance to the mugger.
  correct

1. Running as hard as possible, my breath was hard to catch.

2. Considering her the least likely candidate for the office, I ignored her completely.

3. After having walked in circles for three hours, the way was lost.

4. Being studious at that college, the library was heavily used.

    _____

5. Once cooked, I can enjoy a fine roast.

    _____

6. After I have dined well, I am quite content to sit dreaming at the opera.

    _____

7. Considering everything he has done for the party, his defeat was a complete surprise.

    _____

8. Stuck in traffic for hours, a feeling of despair is no surprise.

    _____

9. While sitting quietly before a wood fire, the noisy children are a nuisance to young and old.

    _____

10. Upon meeting old friends, one's natural response is pleasure.

    _____

INFINITIVES AS ADJECTIVES

Infinitives often function as adjectives.

Consider the following sentences:

> She has the most *to gain* of anyone on the staff.   (The infinitive *to gain* modifies *most*.)
> The way *to proceed* has not been determined.   (The infinitive *to proceed* modifies *way*.)
> Her urge *to pray* was overwhelming.   (The infinitive *to pray* modifies *urge*.)

Infinitive phrases—infinitives together with their modifiers and objects or complements—may also function as adjectives:

> The general ordered his army into action *to defeat the rebel force*.   (The infinitive phrase *to defeat the rebel force* modifies *action*.)
> Samuel Bridge had cutlery *to carve every type of roast*.   (The infinitive phrase *to carve every type of roast* modifies *cutlery*.)
> For his birthday, he was given a device *to use in opening clams*.   (The infinitive phrase *to use in opening clams* modifies *device*.)

15. In the following sentences, underscore the *infinitives* and the *infinitive phrases* used as adjectives and identify the *elements* they modify, as shown in these examples:

> We all have our own lives to lead.   lives
> She wanted permission to arrest the offending motorist.   permission

1. The full jury will surely reconsider its vote to acquit.   _____
2. Well prepared food to suit the happy occasion was served all day long.   _____
3. Fortunate cats have owners to feed them.   _____
4. His work consisted solely of music to dance to.   _____
5. Judy hoped to find a good biography to read.   _____

6. She always had a smart joke to meet every situation. _____
7. The correct tool to use for this job is a rubber mallet. _____
8. The minister gave her parishioners permission to miss Sunday services. _____
9. Eileen predictably said she had no clothes to wear. _____
10. The first reporter to cover the story will get a byline. _____

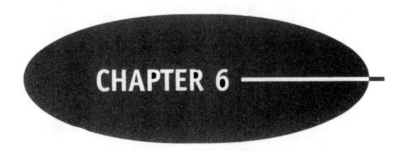

CHAPTER 6

Adverbs

Adverbs modify verbs, adjectives, and other adverbs.

She walked *quickly.*   (The adverb *quickly* modifies the verb *walked.*)

They snored *melodically.*   (The adverb *melodically* modifies the verb *snored.*)

They were *really* unhappy.   (The adverb *really* modifies the adjective *unhappy.*)

My daughters are *completely* fearless.   (The adverb *completely* modifies the adjective *fearless.*)

He plays tennis *very* well.   (The adverb *very* modifies the adverb *well.*)

Children are *almost always* hungry.   (The adverb *almost* modifies *always,* which is an adverb that modifies the adjective *hungry.*)

Adverbs also can modify entire clauses:

Perhaps you are wrong, but I will listen to your claims.   (The adverb *Perhaps* modifies the clause *you are wrong.*)

Surely the train will be on time, but I hope not.   (*Surely* modifies *the train will be on time.*)

Adverbs also can modify all the rest of a sentence:

Perhaps you picked up the wrong hat.

Surely the train will soon be ready for service.

1. In the following sentences, underscore the *adverbs* and identify the elements of the sentences they modify as shown in these examples. Note that there can be more than one adverb in a sentence.

They play their instruments <u>lovingly.</u>   <u>play</u>

<u>Certainly</u> we will come to dinner.   <u>we will come to dinner</u>

I thought she was <u>extremely</u> careful.   <u>careful</u>

She was <u>completely</u> exhausted and <u>thoroughly</u> wet.   <u>exhausted, wet</u>

1. She began to weep quietly when the police officer came to the door.
    _____

2. She was completely honest in her work and in her dealings with everyone.
    _____

3. Ideally, the doctor will have completed her examination. _____

4. Partially closed ears are usually ineffective against quietly spoken gossip.
    _____

5. Although they practice diligently, they never satisfy their teacher. _____

6. He sat patiently through the spectacle but finally withdrew. _____

7. Hazel works quite carefully on her homework. _____

8. Subsequently, we discussed the bill with the manager. _____

9. The district attorney openly rebuked the witness for what was a fairly obvious exaggeration. _____

10. You never can work too carefully. _____

RECOGNIZING ADVERBS

Adverbs Ending in -*ly*

The easiest adverbs to recognize are those that end in -*ly*. The only pitfall to avoid is confusing -*ly* adverbs with -*ly* adjectives. Remember that adjectives modify only nouns and pronouns. Adverbs modify everything else.

The following words are some of the adjectives that end in -*ly*: *comely*, *costly*, *early*, *lively*, *lovely*, *surly*. See how they are used in these sentences:

> A *comely* appearance is always admired.
> *Costly* jewelry is beyond the reach of most students.
> The *early* bird catches the worm.
> The fiddler played a *lively* tune.
> The *lovely* sunset provided a fitting climax to our day.
> The trainer was a *surly* one, all right.

In the first five sentences, the italicized adjectives modify nouns: *appearance*, *jewelry*, *bird*, *tune*, *sunset*. The last italicized adjective, *surly*, modifies *one*, a pronoun.

Adverbs that end in -*ly* are formed by adding -*ly* to an adjective, a present participle, or a past participle.

Adjective	Adverb
beautiful	beautifully
hateful	hatefully
quick	quickly
sure	surely

Present Participle	Adverb
fitting	fittingly
swimming	swimmingly

Present Participle	Adverb
terrifying	terrifyingly
willing	willingly

Past Participle	Adverb
advised	advisedly
affected	affectedly
assured	assuredly
deserved	deservedly

When an adjective ends in *-able* or *-ible*, the adverb is formed by changing the final *e* to *y*: peaceable, *peaceably*; horrible, *horribly*; terrible, *terribly*.

Consider the following sentences:

He regarded her *hatefully.*

Surely they will reconcile their differences.

Rose will *finally* receive her permanent appointment.

They were *terribly* mangled in the accident.

All the italicized words in these sentences perform adverbial functions. *Surely* modifies the entire sentence it appears in. The others modify the verbs in their sentences. They must not be confused with adjectives.

2. In the following sentences, classify the italicized words ending in *-ly* as *adjectives* or *adverbs* as shown in these examples:

The *lively* melody was typical of Schubert.   ___adjective___

A *friendly* gesture is always welcome.   ___adjective___

He regarded the world *hostilely.*   ___adverb___

She closed her program *fittingly* by singing the national anthem.   ___adverb___

1. *Disorderly* conduct is a vague charge that covers many types of actions.   _____

2. The manager closed his first year *successfully.*   _____

3. They went along *unwillingly* to school.   _____

4. He was *slightly* upset by the incident.   _____

5. Most mothers look *lovingly* at their new infants.   _____

6. A *lovely* dessert is a fitting end to a good meal.   _____

7. My sister inferred *correctly* that she was no longer wanted.   _____

8. He looked about him *calmly* and proclaimed his innocence.   _____

9. To everyone's surprise, the expert copy editor made a *costly* error.   _____

10. He will *assuredly* find something to praise in my work.   _____

11. The cat will find its food *eventually.*   _____

12. *Homely* virtues are disappearing from city life.   _____

13. He added *parenthetically* that he was pleased with the overall outcome.   _____

14. The decline in quality was *considerably* greater than we would have liked.   _____

15. One could question whether the statement was *favorably* received.   _____

Recognizing Adverbs by Their Functions

Adverbs answer the following questions: *how? how much? when? where? why? true or false?* We thus can classify adverbs as adverbs of *manner, degree, time, place, cause or purpose,* or *assertion.*

Adverbs of manner answer the question *how?*

> He works *carefully.*
>
> Ruth cooks *well.*

Adverbs of degree answer the question *how much?*

> You are *inadequately* prepared for graduate studies.
>
> He has *completely* exhausted his inheritance.

Adverbs of time answer the question *when?*

> They arrive *late* for most appointments.
>
> She has not played tennis *recently.*

Adverbs of place answer the question *where?*

> He walked *downstairs.*
>
> They went *south* for the winter.

Adverbs of cause or purpose answer the question *why?*

> I will *therefore* quit the team.
>
> She will *consequently* be dismissed.

Adverbs of assertion answer the question *true or false?*

> She will *surely* be hired for the job.
>
> She is *not* acceptable in my home.

3. In the following sentences, underline all *adverbs* and identify their functions—*manner, degree, time, place, cause or purpose, assertion*—as shown in these examples:

> I cannot forgive you <u>completely.</u>   degree
>
> <u>Lately</u> I have had many colds.   time
>
> She <u>certainly</u> is our best speaker.   assertion

1. Teachers sometimes make mistakes in scoring quizzes.   _____
2. I may possibly join the two of you.   _____
3. He almost lost his temper.   _____
4. He fell awkwardly to the kitchen floor and fainted.   _____
5. Men never make passes at girls who wear glasses.   _____
6. He lived frugally during bad times.   _____
7. Finally our train arrived, two hours behind schedule.   _____
8. Have you ever gone there?   _____
9. He has been paid less than I from his first day on the job.   _____
10. The bus you must take leaves soon.   _____
11. Yes, I will go to sleep.   _____
12. You will undoubtedly be reprimanded.   _____

13. I am guardedly optimistic. _____
14. You must move quickly if you are to succeed. _____
15. Go west, young man. _____

DISTINGUISHING ADVERBS FROM ADJECTIVES

Many words in English function both as adjectives and as adverbs. The surest way to tell whether a particular word is an adjective or an adverb in a given sentence is to determine what its function is in the sentence. For this you must go back to the fundamental distinction between an adjective and an adverb: adjectives modify nouns and pronouns; adverbs modify everything else.

The following list supplies some of the words that are used both as adjectives and adverbs:

bad	fast	right
better	first	rough
bright	hard	second
cheap	high	sharp
close	late	slow
deep	little	smooth
doubtless	loose	straight
early	loud	third
enough	low	tight
even	much	well
fair	near	worse
far	quick	wrong

Many of these words also have forms ending in *-ly*: *badly, brightly, cheaply, deeply,* etc. The *-ly* forms are preferred in formal English by some grammarians and, in many instances, are used exclusively in certain idiomatic constructions.

Consider the following sentences:

The arrow fell *close* to the mark.
Watch them *closely*.
She practices *hard* all day.
She could *hardly* bend her fingers.

In both pairs of sentences, the modifiers *close, closely, hard,* and *hardly* perform adverbial functions. *Close* modifies the verb *fell*. *Closely* modifies the verb *watch*. *Hard* modifies the verb *practices*. *Hardly* modifies the verb *bend*. Thus, they are all adverbs.

By contrast, *close* and *hard* are used as adjectives in the following sentences:

Close work strains my eyes.
Hard times will soon be upon us.

Close modifies the noun *work*. *Hard* modifies the noun *times*. Thus, they both are adjectives here. Of course, *closely* and *hardly* are never used as adjectives.

4. In the following sentences, identify the italicized modifiers as *adjectives* or *adverbs* as shown in these examples:

> She was a *bad* writer.   <u>adjective</u>
>
> He will *doubtless* be fired.   <u>adverb</u>

1. Drive *slow* if you want to enjoy your vacation trip.   _____
2. He was *much* better at bridge than I was.   _____
3. *Even* a small amount of that chemical will hurt you.   _____
4. He was an *even-tempered* man.   _____
5. We went to see her *late* in the afternoon after the baby had been born.   _____
6. She was *fair* and well groomed.   _____
7. You can easily learn to swim *well* when you have a good instructor.   _____
8. Are you sure you are *well*?   _____
9. Are there *enough* knives and forks to set the table for dinner?   _____
10. She slept *enough* for two.   _____
11. I hope you have *better* luck in Las Vegas next time.   _____
12. I was *better* rested that afternoon.   _____
13. He was a *smooth* talker.   _____
14. The table top ultimately was as *smooth* as I could make it.   _____
15. Try *harder* and you will have all the success you wish.   _____

COMPARISON OF ADVERBS

Like adjectives, adverbs have three comparative forms—*absolute, comparative,* and *superlative*—to indicate greater or lesser degrees of the characteristics described.

Adverbs that are identical with adjectives form their comparatives and superlatives in the same manner: *bad, worse, worst; well, better, best,* etc. Even when the absolute form of an adverb ends in *-ly,* the comparative and superlative are identical with the corresponding forms of the adjective: *badly, worse, worst.*

Adverbs also add *-er* and *-est* to the absolute to make their comparatives and superlatives: *deep, deeper, deepest; deeply, deeper, deepest.*

Adverbs also employ *more* and *most* before the absolute form to express the comparative and superlative degrees: *timidly, more timidly, most timidly; happily, more happily, most happily. More* and *most* are commonly used with adverbs containing more than one syllable.

The dictionary is the ultimate authority for the comparison of adverbs. When in doubt, consult your dictionary.

5. In the following sentences, supply the proper *comparative* or *superlative* form of the adverb enclosed in parentheses as shown in these examples:

> Of all the boys, Corky stayed under water (long).   <u>longest</u>
>
> She felt the loss (keenly) than her sister, because she was closer to the child.
>   <u>more keenly</u>

1. Jon slept (comfortably) than she, because he had worked hard all day. _____
2. The bird life in the tropics affected him (deep) than the wildlife in Vermont. _____
3. She certainly treated her sisters (lovingly) than they treated her. _____
4. Rembrandt painted (vividly) than Delacroix. _____
5. Of all the Impressionists, Renoir painted (colorfully). _____
6. Dorothy took (long) to dress than she or her husband expected. _____
7. Your poodle eats (hungrily) than any other dog I ever have seen. _____
8. The women's sixty-yard dash was the (hotly) contested race of the entire afternoon. _____
9. The school bus is the (heavily) overloaded of all the buses on this route. _____
10. Some say the role is so passionately portrayed that the play will be the (heavily) patronized offering of the season. _____

NOUNS AND PHRASES USED AS ADVERBS

Nouns and phrases are often used as adverbs, particularly to indicate time and degree.

She stayed home *evenings*.　(The verb *stayed* is modified by the noun *evenings*.)

I would like to practice *mornings*.　(The infinitive *to practice* is modified by the noun *mornings*.)

They jogged *a mile*.　(The verb *jogged* is modified by the noun phrase *a mile*.)

He swam *two hundred meters*, which was more than any other swimmer could manage. (The verb *swam* is modified by the noun phrase *two hundred meters*.)

He swam *two hundred meters* farther than any other swimmer.　(The adverb *farther* is modified by the noun phrase *two hundred meters*.)

The suit is not worth *four hundred dollars*.　(The adjective *worth* is modified by the noun phrase *four hundred dollars*.)

She always worked *in the morning*.　(The verb *worked* is modified by the prepositional phrase *in the morning*.)

6. In the following sentences, underline the *nouns* and *phrases* used as *adverbs* as shown in the following examples:

   Have you ever seen New York the New York way?
   He decided not to go to the beach.

   1. All the children had been warned not to walk beyond the last house on their street.
   2. Coleridge wrote mornings.
   3. Coleridge wrote in the morning.
   4. In the cool evenings, they usually walked after dinner.
   5. Vermeer continued to paint in the Flemish manner.
   6. They paid seventy dollars at the box office.
   7. Sundays they always watched football games on television.
   8. They waited ten minutes and then launched their attack.

9.   That house costs five hundred thousand dollars.

10.   She weighed twenty pounds more than her younger sister.

ADVERBIAL CLAUSES

Adverbial clauses modify *verbs*, *adverbs*, and *adjectives*, but they most often modify other *clauses*.

Adverbial clauses are best classified according to the type of modification they provide: *cause*, *comparison*, *concession*, *condition*, *manner*, *place*, *purpose*, *result*, and *time*.

Cause—introduced by *as, because, since*:

As there was no other way to accomplish her purpose, she finally announced her decision.   (The adverbial clause answers the question *why?* It modifies the entire main clause.)

We went home *because there was nothing else to do.*   (The adverbial clause answers the question *why?* It modifies the entire main clause.)

Comparison—introduced by *as* and *than*:

Nuclear energy is as expensive *as fossil energy.*   (The verb *is* is understood in the adverbial clause *as fossil energy* [is]. The adverbial clause modifies the adjective *expensive*.)

That car will cost more *than I want to pay.*   (The adverbial clause modifies the adverb *more*.)

Concession—introduced by *although, even if, even though, though*:

Although I remain poor, I am quite content.   (The adverbial clause modifies the entire main clause.)

I shall attend the concert *even though I can ill afford it.*   (The adverbial clause modifies the entire main clause.)

Condition—introduced by *if, on condition that, provided that, unless*:

I shall be glad to conclude this agreement *if you are willing to make small concessions on some of the terms.*   (The adverbial clause modifies the entire main clause.)

They offered to go *on condition that we supply the food and drink.*   (The adverbial clause modifies the entire main clause.)

Had she given her consent earlier, we would have complied as well.   (The adverbial clause modifies the verb *would have complied*. The subject and verb in the adverbial clause are inverted—*had she* instead of *she had*.)

Manner—introduced by *as, as if, as though*:

Corporate officers act *as they are instructed to act.*   (The adverbial clause modifies the verb *act* in the main clause.)

He runs *as if the devil were after him.*   (The adverbial clause modifies the verb *runs*.)

Place—introduced by *where, wherever*:

Where the bee sucks, there suck I.   (The adverbial clause modifies the adverb *there*.)

I meet them *wherever I go.*   (The adverbial clause modifies the entire main clause.)

Purpose—introduced by *in order that, so, that*:

We prepared dinner early *in order that the team would not be held up.*   (The adverbial clause modifies the entire main clause.)

We sent him to college *so he could earn a good living and lead a full life.*   (The adverbial clause modifies the main clause.)

Result—introduced by *so, that*:

The electricity had been turned off, *so we shivered all night.*   (The adverbial clause modifies the entire main clause.)

She delayed so many years *that he grew tired of waiting.*   (The adverbial clause modifies the entire main clause.)

Time—introduced by *after, as, before, since, when, while, until*:

After dinner was finished, she picked up her hat and left.   (The adverbial clause modifies the verbs *picked* and *left.*)

While I was walking downtown, I met Harriet and Clara.   (The adverbial clause modifies the verb *met.*)

7. In the following sentences, underscore the *adverbial clauses* and indicate their *functions* and what they modify, as shown in these examples:

She received preferential treatment <u>though her grades were poor.</u>
    concession—modifies main clause

We have been attending classes <u>since the term began.</u>
    time—modifies verb *have been attending*

1. The air was so fetid that I could no longer remain in the room.

2. Had I paid adequate attention in class, I surely would have done better on the final examination.

3. As always, Felix behaved as if he did not care at all about my feelings.

4. Faulkner is still considered a more profound novelist than most of his contemporaries.

5. Cindy was allowed to stay out late provided that she signed the dormitory register upon leaving.

6. You will soon find a gas station wherever you drive in New Jersey.

7. I had to register for the draft because I had reached the age of eighteen.

8. The student would not submit even though the plagiarism committee questioned him all day.

9. Before you gather up your books, be certain your notes are complete.

10. Since a quorum is not present, votes will not be taken.

11. Although he tried every trick he knew, he could not manage to put the side out.

12. If no one shows up for the picnic, I will give the food to the poor.

   _____

13. I lost the heel of my right shoe as I was crossing the street.

   _____

14. I never again had as good a record as I had in my first term.

   _____

15. Had I remembered what the instructor told me, I would have finished the final examination with time to spare.

   _____

16. Under the stress of a dog show, puppies do not behave as their masters have taught them.

   _____

17. Because there was nothing left to do but surrender, the troops laid down their arms.

   _____

18. I am permitted to leave my station whenever I can find a replacement.

   _____

19. Open admissions is a splendid policy if colleges maintain their academic standards.

   _____

20. I have been in this room only once since it was painted.

   _____

21. She pleaded almost inaudibly as if she was thoroughly exhausted.

   _____

22. Since there are only four of us, why not play bridge instead of poker?

   _____

23. Although nothing appeared to be wrong with the car, it would not start.

   _____

24. Wherever I go in New York, I meet old friends.

   _____

25. While I was having my lunch, a friend dropped by my table.

   _____

CONJUNCTIVE ADVERBS

Conjunctive adverbs are adverbs used as conjunctions. (Conjunctions are treated in Chapter 7.) They join elements of a sentence and affect meaning in a way that ordinary conjunctions cannot:

The committee had formally rejected his application; *however,* he immediately decided to exercise his right of appeal.   (While *however* joins two independent clauses, it indicates a relationship between the clauses that is not indicated by the most commonly used conjunctions: *and, or, but,* etc. The word *however* is a conjunctive adverb.)

Hillary relinquished her position as chairman of the group; *moreover,* she severed all connection with the party that sponsored the group.   (Again, *moreover,* a conjunctive adverb, joins two independent clauses, but indicates a special relationship between the two clauses.)

This use of conjunctive adverbs between independent clauses requires a semicolon before the conjunctive adverb and a comma after it as shown in the two examples above.

When conjunctive adverbs are placed within a clause, commas are used to set them off:

She will, *therefore*, establish her identity before the formal interrogation begins.   (This use of a conjunctive adverb suggests that something has been said in the preceding sentence that justifies the use of *therefore*. For example, the preceding sentence could have been: *The rules of interrogation are quite rigorous in demanding that the witness be identified fully. She will, therefore, establish* etc.)

When used at the beginning of a sentence, a conjunctive adverb is set off by a comma:

The rules of interrogation are quite rigorous in demanding that the witness be identified fully. *Therefore*, she will establish her identity before the interrogation begins.

The most common conjunctive adverbs are: *accordingly, also, anyhow, besides, consequently, furthermore, hence, henceforth, however, indeed, instead, likewise, meanwhile, moreover, namely, nevertheless, otherwise, still, therefore,* and *thus*.

8. Punctuate the following sentences as shown in these examples:

The United States celebrated its bicentennial in 1976; meanwhile, many cities and towns celebrated their tricentennials.

The experience gained in that war should have proved conclusively that colonial wars always end in disaster; many nations, nevertheless, pursue policies that lead to war far from their shores.

1. I insist on going to the baseball game I insist moreover that you go with me.

2. The organization treasury is completely empty it will nevertheless continue to attempt to raise funds so that it can pay its debts.

3. The final date for submittal of proposals has not yet passed we will therefore receive all properly executed offers until that date arrives.

4. Complete agreement between the two contestants is not likely however we can always hope that both parties will somehow see that their interests lie in mutual trust.

5. The patient shows no signs of recovering despite all the medical treatment he has been given thus there is nothing to do but hope that careful nursing and the processes of nature will see him through.

INTENSIFIERS

Certain adverbs, such as *certainly, extremely, highly, least, much, quite, somewhat, such, too, tremendously,* and *very*, are used to emphasize the meaning of an adjective or adverb. These adverbs are classified as *intensifiers*. Intensifiers may do little to enrich adjectives and adverbs that are already meaningful. When deciding whether to use an intensifier in a sentence you are writing, read the sentence first with the intensifier and then without it. Consider whether the intensifier adds to meaning.

Consider the following sentences:

She is a *very* pretty girl.   (Does *very* add much to *pretty*?)

I am not *too* interested in his remarks.   (Why not say *I am not interested* or *I am uninterested*?)

Yet, intensifiers sometimes convey important meaning:

> I am *too* fat to get into my clothes.
> He is *too* big for his britches.

The message is clear: use intensifiers when they add significantly to meaning; omit them when they do not.

9. Underscore the *intensifiers* in the following sentences and indicate whether they should be kept or deleted, as shown in these examples:

> I had <u>such</u> trouble finding my way. ___delete___
> He is the <u>least</u> likely candidate for that office. ___keep___

1. Her teachers found her to be an extremely capable student. _____
2. He found himself suffering much the same poverty he had known before entering graduate school. _____
3. This color scheme is too violent for my taste. _____
4. I am somewhat embarrassed by all the attention I have been getting. _____
5. The crowd was tremendously fascinated by the fine addresses delivered that day. _____
6. I am extremely eager to continue until the year 2010. _____
7. This car is quite new in design, but it still makes bad mileage. _____
8. I am very sorry our beloved professor has died. _____
9. I was quite disappointed in my grades. _____
10. You are too beautiful for words. _____

INFINITIVES AS ADVERBS

Infinitives and infinitive phrases function as adverbs in many sentences:

> Edward knows French well enough *to pass as a Frenchman.* (The infinitive phrase *to pass as a Frenchman* modifies the adverb *enough.*)
> The Senator returned to Maine *to campaign for reelection.* (The infinitive phrase *to campaign for reelection* modifies the verb *returned.*)
> He works *to survive* and reads *to live.* (The infinitive *to survive* modifies the verb *works.* The infinitive *to live* modifies *reads.*)

10. In the following sentences, underscore the *infinitives* and *infinitive phrases* used as adverbs, and identify the elements they modify as shown in these examples:

> The Yugoslavian diplomat felt confident enough <u>to return home.</u> ___enough___
> They sold <u>to realize a profit.</u> ___sold___

1. Jerry tends to become violent when he is frustrated. _____
2. The storm seems to cover several Southern states. _____
3. Resolutions were introduced to repeal the abortion laws. _____

4. He bats left-handed to utilize his great speed. _____

5. She didn't dare mock anyone; she was too gentle a person. _____

6. They intend to travel to Scotland again this summer. _____

7. Dogs are inclined to drink a great deal of water. _____

8. The landlord tried to evict his objectionable tenant. _____

9. Librarians are eager to stock their shelves with worthwhile books. _____

10. Most adolescents love to travel on their own. _____

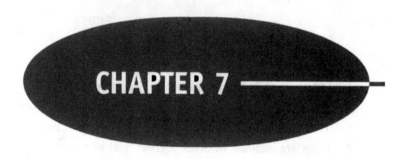

CHAPTER 7

Prepositions and Conjunctions

PREPOSITIONS

A preposition is a word that conveys a meaning of *position*, *direction*, *time*, or other *abstraction*. It serves to relate its object to another sentence element.

A prepositional phrase consists of a preposition, its object, and any modifiers of the object. In the prepositional phrase *by the greatest German musician*, the preposition is *by*, the object is *musician*, and the modifiers of the object are *the greatest German*.

Prepositional phrases are used to modify *verbs*, *nouns*, *pronouns*, and *adjectives*:

Relating to Verbs

> She found the sleeping child *in her room.*   (Where did she find the sleeping child? *In her room.*)
> They stored their files *under the table.*   (Where did they store their files? *Under the table.*)

Relating to Nouns and Pronouns

> She felt the hatred *of the entire family.*   (Whose hatred? The hatred *of the entire family.*)
> I want anything *by that author.*   (What do I want *by that author? Anything.*)

Relating to Adjectives

> She was young *in heart.*   (Young in what sense? Young *in heart.*)
> The book was considered profane *in intent.*   (In what sense profane? Profane *in intent.*)

The nine most commonly used prepositions are: *at, by, for, from, in, of, on, to,* and *with.* There are many more, and you will shortly be given a list of other frequently used prepositions.

1. In the following sentences, underscore all *prepositional phrases* as shown in these examples:

> We have worked hard all week <u>for our cause.</u>
> We went <u>to the store</u> yesterday <u>at noon.</u>

1. She was treated for hepatitis by the doctor.
2. I'm just a little girl from Little Rock.
3. She often goes to the theater with her father.
4. The Gardners will be at the seashore during the entire summer.
5. I hope you reach the airport in time for the late flight.
6. On two occasions, you have forgotten your appointment with the dentist.
7. For all we know, life will never be the same.
8. The trees are alive with color in the autumn.
9. There are three people in the house who will stay for lunch.
10. This money will be reserved for charitable purposes.

2. In the following sentences, identify the *prepositions* and the *objects of prepositions* as shown in these examples:

> The surgeon operated <u>for</u> <u>appendicitis</u>.
> They went <u>to</u> the <u>planetarium</u> <u>in</u> <u>time</u> <u>for</u> the afternoon <u>showing</u>.

1. He considers price increases a precursor of economic recession.
2. Your enthusiasm for hard work is not the greatest.
3. Some of my friends will not be at the next reunion.
4. The postal service has not delivered the mail for which I have been waiting.
5. She went to the stadium once again in dread of a boring afternoon.
6. A symphony by Beethoven is always a fresh experience.
7. She went from the nursery to the emergency care room.
8. Daffodils tell us of the arrival of spring, but say nothing of how cold spring can be.
9. Literature was one of her favorite studies, yet she was also fond of the sciences.
10. We shall be leaving for Antarctica in a few months.

3. In the following sentences underscore the *prepositional phrases* and identify the *verbs, nouns, pronouns*, or *adjectives* modified, as shown in these examples:

> His respect <u>for his elders</u> was apparent.   *respect* (noun)
> Few <u>of the later poems</u> show any special qualities.   *Few* (pronoun)

1. During the raid three guards were wounded. _____
2. They lost their purses in the bus station. _____
3. I removed my hat as the flag passed by the reviewing stand. _____
4. By the end of the performance, no one was left in the audience. _____
5. Close to our school is a new public housing development. _____
6. He was rewarded for his courtesy by the old woman. _____
7. He took great delight in his coin collection. _____
8. Is this the most direct way to the hospital? _____
9. Elementary decency is never recognized by some people. _____
10. She selected her European itinerary with great care. _____

Commonly Used Prepositions

The following list identifies those prepositions most commonly encountered; it is by no means complete. Among the words listed here are the nine prepositions that were given previously. In addition to the single words that constitute most of the entries in this list, there are some phrases that function as prepositions: *in back of*, *in addition to*, etc.

With each entry in the list, two phrases are supplied to illustrate use of the prepositions.

aboard   aboard the ship, aboard the airplane
about   about town, about people
above   above all, above my head
according to   according to the newspapers, according to custom
across   across the way, across our front yard
after   after a while, after meals
against   against public opinion, against the wall
ahead of   ahead of the crowd, ahead of his time
along   along the street, along the route
alongside   alongside the caravan, alongside the prison
amid   amid our preparations, amid our activity
amidst   amidst all my activity, amidst the local people
among   among other things, among the crowd
apart from   apart from my own feelings, apart from the expense involved
around   around the corner, around her waist
as far as   as far as Washington, as far as the train depot
aside from   aside from his published writings, aside from my own thoughts
as to   as to the point you raised, as to the performance itself
at   at no point, at the final moment
back of   back of the bus, back of the objection
because of   because of his poverty, because of our complete apathy
before   before dinner, before leaving
behind   behind his smile, behind closed doors
behind in   behind in the rent, behind in his payments
below   below the roof, below the living room
beneath   beneath my standards, beneath respect
beside   beside a garden wall, beside herself
besides   besides the dean himself, besides the immediate family
between   between you and me, between July and September
beyond   beyond my ken, beyond the mountains
but   but me, but a handful of people
by   by the same writer, by tomorrow
concerning   concerning taste, concerning her obstinacy
contrary to   contrary to my advice, contrary to the Constitution
despite   despite all our best efforts, despite his lateness
down   down the stairs, down the street
due to   due to lack of sleep, due to habitual absences
during   during his tenure, during the Bush years
except   except me, except my brother
for   for your own safety, for the sake of God
from   from nowhere, from the western sky
in   in back, in expectation
in addition to   in addition to her efforts, in addition to AIDS

in back of in back of the house, in back of her mind
in front of in front of it, in front of the store
in lieu of in lieu of loving care, in lieu of a full-time chairman
in light of in light of her accomplishments, in light of the child's age
in place of in place of the flowers, in place of the current exhibit
in regard to in regard to your letter, in regard to her request
inside inside his head, inside the vault
in spite of in spite of his mother's request, in spite of his good intentions
instead of instead of the marines, instead of going home
into into a deep depression, into the French quarter
in view of in view of her prejudices, in view of your demands
like like a bee, like an angel
near near the old house, near despair
of of pioneer stock, of great reputation
off off the roof, off his outstanding debt
on on my account, on occasion
on account of on account of the delay, on account of the inconvenience
on board on board the ocean liner, on board the Orient Express
onto onto the platform, onto her shoulders
out out the door, out the window
out of out of sight and out of mind, out of the hall
over over your head, over the party
owing to owing to your anxiety, owing to his eagerness
past past the school yard, past my comprehension
per per second, per minute
round round the barnyard, round my head
since since her death, since the turn of the century
through through my thoughts, through the gate
throughout throughout her life, throughout the night
till till death, till today
to to no purpose, to New York
toward toward better understanding, toward late afternoon
towards towards New York, towards the north
under under two flags, under suspicion
until until morning, until death
unto unto each other, unto ourselves
up up the staircase, up the wall
upon upon well-founded suspicions, upon further thought
up to up to now, up to the limit of his ability
via via the Alcan Highway, via Route 66
with with care, with no friends
within within his hearing, within the time
without without arms, without assistance

4. In the following sentences, underline the *prepositional phrases* as shown in these examples:

He was seen smoking <u>behind the barn</u>.

The laptop computer I wanted was <u>out of stock</u>.

1. Throughout the term, he found her behavior utterly incomprehensible.
2. He turned the problem into a major exercise.

3. The Mercedes swerved past the guardrail and onto the lawn.

4. Italian vintners are known for their inexpensive white and red wines.

5. Across town there is a little restaurant that serves food like that of France.

6. Your request will be granted if it is within reason.

7. Because of his delay in paying, electrical service has been terminated.

8. Out of the pitch black night came a creature of threatening appearance.

9. Margaret lived near the city center, but she played no part in city life.

10. They swept past the maître d'hôtel and demanded to be seated near the band.

11. The actress fell off the stage and broke one of her legs.

12. Since her husband's death, Paula had had no life of her own.

13. If you agree, I shall go instead of you.

14. In spite of everything you say, I am sure you had a good time.

15. He went straight toward the bar, despite my repeated warnings.

Object of Preposition

The object of a preposition is always in the objective case.

> He gave the book *to me.*   (The object of the preposition *to* is the pronoun *me*, which is in the objective case.)
>
> *Whom* did you give the book *to?*   (*Whom* is the object of the preposition *to* and is in the objective case.)

Despite the tendency of many speakers and writers to use *who* when *whom* is preferred, as in the second sample sentence, anyone interested in good grammar should use *whom* as the objective form of the pronoun *who*.

5. In the following sentences, supply the proper forms of the *pronouns* as shown in these examples:

> I found the child with (he)   __him__
>
> If you won't do this for (she), (who) will you do it for?   __her, whom__

1. Do you think anyone but (she) can do it? _____

2. I will not go to see you if you have her with (you). _____

3. Shirley told him she would give the present to (we). _____

4. The committee decided to award the plaque to (whoever) I choose. _____

5. I shall go with (she) when she calls upon (they). _____

6. If you lack confidence in (they), why don't you say so? _____

7. Ruskin had admiration for (he) as a painter. _____

8. William addressed his letter to (she) because he knew no one else on the committee. _____

9. (Who) are you referring to? _____

10. The letter you sent has been forwarded to (I) at the address I gave (she). _____

Differentiating Prepositions from Other Parts of Speech

Many prepositions, such as *after*, *but*, *for*, and *since*, are also used as adverbs, adjectives, or conjunctions. The way to differentiate the various uses of these words is to examine the roles they play in a sentence.

Consider the following sentences:

> The ducks were in a row, one *after* another.   (preposition)
>
> Do not follow *after* him.   (preposition)
>
> Have you inquired *after* her?   (preposition)
>
> *After* dinner we were treated to cups of superb coffee.   (preposition)
>
> She was named *after* her aunt.   (preposition)
>
> Jill came *after.*   (adverb)
>
> They lived happily ever *after.*   (adverb)
>
> The *after* years often are terrible.   (adjective)
>
> *After* I find the place I want, I shall buy it and settle down.   (conjunction)

In the above examples, *after*, when used as an adverb or an adjective, directly modifies a word or words: *came after*, *lived after*, *after years*. In the sentence in which *after* is used as a conjunction, it is followed by a clause: *After I find the place I want.* When used as a preposition, *after* introduces a prepositional phrase: *after another*, *after him*, *after her*, *after dinner*, *after her aunt*.

6.   In the following sentences, underline the *prepositions*, if any, as shown in these examples:

> This has been the warmest winter <u>since</u> 1940.
>
> She has since left this part <u>of</u> the country.
>
> <u>After</u> her departure I have not been the same.

1.   She will not be eligible, for she has not paid taxes here.

2.   She will compete for the prize, since it represents her fondest dream.

3.   We all agreed that no one but her can even be considered.

4.   Alice began to shout for joy, but soon stopped because of her irritated throat.

5.   They have an eye for beauty, but whatever they choose to paint pleases no one with any taste.

6.   They followed closely after, but no matter how hard they tried, the thief got away.

7.   I have not seen anything of him since.

8.   After the ball was over, many a heart was broken.

9.   He followed after her dutifully, wishing nothing else but her happiness.

10.   For all we know, we may never meet again.

Prepositional Phrases as Modifiers

Prepositional phrases function as adverbs or adjectives. Consider the following sentences:

> We decided *at the last minute.*   (adverb modifying *decided*)
>
> They come *from Puerto Rico.*   (adverb modifying *come*)

Most government officials speak *with caution.*   (adverb modifying *speak*)
The family vacationed *in Saratoga Springs.*   (adverb modifying *vacationed*)
People *of quality* do not gossip all the time.   (adjective modifying *People*)
The family *in mourning* wore black clothing.   (adjective modifying *family*)
The hero *as anti-hero* characterizes American detective fiction.   (adjective modifying *hero*)
Training *in martial arts* has never lost its popularity.   (adjective modifying *Training*)

7. In the following sentences, identify the *italicized prepositional phrases* as *adverbs* or *adjectives*
as shown in these examples:

She was recognized *as a leader.*   adverb
The picture *in the window* was stunning.   adjective
We dined *in an elegant restaurant.*   adverb

1. *On Thursdays* I dine alone *in a modest restaurant*, hoping to have complete privacy.
   _____

2. A house *in a neighborhood* that is well maintained will always appreciate *in value.*
   _____

3. He behaved *in a manner* that can charitably be described *as poor taste.*
   _____

4. Her attitude *toward the excellent job offer* staggered those of us who, *like her*, were usually
   unemployed. _____

5. The sailor *in dress uniform* sauntered *into the cafe* and ordered a glass *of milk.*
   _____

6. The traditional attitude *towards graduate studies* has shifted somewhat *in light of increasing
   salaries.* _____

7. The trees *behind our school* need professional care *for survival.* _____

8. Can you manage to inspect and repair our plumbing *in a single visit?*
   _____

9. Little *in this world* can be accomplished *without hard work.* _____

10. The only flaw *in his solution* is that he has completely overlooked the best *of clues.*
    _____

8. In the following sentences, underscore all *prepositional phrases*, if any, as shown in these
examples:

When my clothes need laundering, I take them <u>to the automatic laundry</u> <u>for quick and
inexpensive washing</u>, but I usually cannot afford to use the dryers, so I put my washed
clothes <u>on a line.</u>

<u>Besides hoping</u>, there was little I could do, since nothing was left <u>of the money.</u>

1. Of all the members, she is the first I would accuse of doing such mischief.

2. The cottage stood on a little hill behind the wall, waiting for someone to come along and
buy it.

3. Paper is wasted in offices that are equipped with copying machines.

4. A pipe filled with good tobacco can help a lonely man.

5. Near the farm stood three unused kilns once devoted to the making of lime.

6. A maple tree will give sweet sap if the nights are cold and the days are warm.

7. She stood by the firehouse, wondering whether the alarm would ring during her lunch hour so she could see how quickly the handsome firemen would respond.

8. In the afternoons, he would walk about the city, looking for some diversion that would cheer him in his misery.

9. The apartment was filled with smoke after the firemen stopped spraying their water on the upper floors.

10. Once he had completed his essay, he left the library and walked home.

11. The trees were in full leaf and looked as though they were happy that spring had come.

12. I had to spend most of my time on chores that left little evidence of completion once they were done.

13. Children, as we all know, often find amusement in tormenting younger children.

14. For days on end, the pair worked to repair the damage to the sidewalk.

15. In the afternoons, she found that the sunlight was too strong for her eyes, which were more accustomed to the subdued light of the nursing home where she worked.

CONJUNCTIONS

Conjunctions connect words, phrases, or clauses. They are classified as *coordinating* or *subordinating*. Subordinating conjunctions join only clauses. Coordinating conjunctions join words, phrases, and clauses:

He *and* I, She *or* I   (coordinating conjunctions joining words)

The chair in the living room *and* the one in the den; the red car *or* the blue car (coordinating conjunctions joining phrases)

She has been nominated, *but* I hope she will withdraw.   (coordinating conjunction joining clauses)

There still is time to get to the game, *for* we have fifteen minutes.   (coordinating conjunction joining clauses)

The most common coordinating conjunctions are *and, but, for, nor, or, so,* and *yet.* (*So* and *yet* sometimes act as subordinating conjunctions.)

Other conjunctions classified as coordinating are the so-called *correlatives*, which occur in pairs: *either...or, neither...nor, not only...but, not only...but also,* and *both...and*:

Either you leave at once *or* I shall call the police.

Neither Jane *nor* Alice deserves to be considered for promotion.

Not only has the nation suffered domestically, *but* our reputation abroad is poor.

Not only does she write maudlin novels, *but* she *also* writes bathetic poetry.

Both coffee *and* tea were drunk to excess.

As can be seen, coordinating conjunctions are used to connect sentence elements that have equivalent value.

Subordinating conjunctions connect sentence elements—clauses—of less than equal value. The most common subordinating conjunctions are *after, although, as, as if, as long as, because, before, how,*

if, in order that, since, so, so that, though, till, unless, until, when, where, wherever, while, why, and *yet.*
The relative pronouns *that, what, which,* and *who* also act as subordinating conjunctions.

The following sentences show some uses of subordinating conjunctions:

I will take care of her *after* the doctor has gone.

I cannot take all the blame, *although* I will accept partial responsibility.

They arrived in our town *before* the others did.

They have been studying Latin *since* they entered second grade.

There comes a time *when* all bills must be paid.

Richard sat in the library *while* Jon was out on the playing field.

9. In the following sentences underscore the *conjunctions* and indicate whether they are
coordinating or *subordinating* as shown in these examples:

Helen worked as an engineer <u>and</u> designer, <u>while</u> her husband continued his graduate
studies.
      coordinating, subordinating

He enjoyed working on the farm, <u>but</u> his wife objected to the strenuous <u>and</u> lonely life.
      coordinating, coordinating

1. Not only have we wasted our health, but we have lost the will to live.

2. I did all this so that our children might have better lives.

3. Since you left home, everything has been the same except for the deteriorating condition
of your room and the increasing cost of feeding the family.

4. Until you find you have work to do and responsibilities to meet, you cannot say you have
reached adult status.

5. Either the husband or the wife will have to make peace with the other, because life is much
too hectic with both of them forever fighting.

6. When you decide to submit your complete manuscript, please let me know so I can arrange
to have you paid.

7. The chair you gave me has no springs or cover, yet it has a charm all of its own.

8. Henry or Deirdre will have to be present when we select a delegate to the national
convention.

9. So there will be no misunderstanding, let me explain that we all must work together and
choose our words carefully in addressing one another.

10. Wherever the job takes us, we must be prepared to go, without complaining or claiming
that we were kept in the dark.

Answers

1. 1. Verb *receive*, Subject, *Playwrights*, *authors*, Direct object *acclaim*, Complement none
2. Verb *preserve*, Subject *Libraries*, Direct object *wisdom*, Complement none
3. Verb *are*, Subject *stores*, Direct object *none*, Complement *busiest*
4. Verb *has*, Subject *Buenos Aires*, Direct object *house*, Complement none
5. Verb *is*, Subject *Religion*, Direct object *none*, Complement *course*
6. Verb *were*, Subject *Eli*, *Samuel*, Direct object *none*, Complement *prophets*
7. Verb *have produced*, Subject *Wars*, Direct object *death*, *destruction*, Complement none
8. Verb *telephoned*, Subject *Tamara*, Direct object *brothers*, Complement none
9. Verb *served*, Subject *waiter*, Direct object *water*, Complement none
10. Verb *was ransacked*, Subject *dormitory*, Direct object *none*, Complement none
11. Verb *were ransacking*, Subject *Burglars*, Direct object *dormitory*, Complement none
12. Verb *studied*, Subject *Helen*, Direct object *Italian*, Complement none
13. Verb *felt*, Subject *She*, Direct object *lining*, Complement none
14. Verb *felt*, Subject *He*, Direct object *none*, Complement *well*
15. Verb *called*, Subject *defendants*, Direct object *lawyer*, Complement none
16. Verb *ensures*, Subject *mind*, Direct object *success*, Complement none
17. Verb *have revolutionized*, Subject *Microchips*, Direct object *industry*, Complement none
18. Verb *is*, Subject *bibliography*, Direct object *none*, Complement *list*
19. Verb *carry*, Subject *teenagers*, Direct object *telephones*, Complement none
20. Verb *wear*, Subject *professionals*, Direct object *hats*, Complement none
21. Verb *suited*, Subject *shirt*, *tie*, Direct object *him*, Complement none
22. Verb *are respected*, Subject *matadors*, Direct object *none*, Complement none
23. Verb *are air conditioned*, Subject *homes*, Direct object *none*, Complement none
24. Verb *cleans*, *cools*, Subject *Air conditioning*, Direct object *buildings*, Complement none
25. Verb *wrote*, Subject *Conrad*, Direct object *none*, Complement none

2. 1. vacationers, 2. museum, 3. clients, 4. customer, 5. him, 6. museum, 7. judges, 8. Marie, 9. roommates, 10. British Museum, 11. him, 12. readers, 13. witnesses, 14. clients, 15. parents

3. 1. outdoor, enthusiastic; 2. patient, joyfully; 3. tired, very, late; 4. tasty, spaghetti, always; 5. regularly, serviced, safer; 6. large, carefully; 7. neighborhood, early, late; 8. always, clean, neatly; 9. never, news; 10. Our, best, almost; 11. tonight; 12. Our, weekly, only, local; 13. nighttime, old; 14. never, broken; 5. White, roast; 16. Herman's, good, dance; 17. Bertha's, blue; 18. never, before; 19. tall, gently, frightened; 20. Please, two, sharp; 21. red, slowly; 22. stormy, high; 23. Happy, hard; 24. Robert's, old, new; 25. million, annually

4. 1. <u>that the champion wore</u>, <u>on the tennis court</u>, <u>with green piping</u>; 2. <u>in the ski mask</u>, <u>down the stairs</u>; 3. <u>on cold nights</u>, <u>without a coat</u>; 4. <u>of the visiting team</u>, <u>around right end</u>; 5. <u>in which we are living</u>; 6. <u>that is double parked</u>, <u>in the entire street</u>; 7. <u>carrying the brown portfolio</u>, <u>on his desk</u>; 8. <u>across the sidewalk</u>; 9. <u>of all ages</u>; 10. <u>on the corner</u>, <u>from many cities</u>; 11. <u>of unemployed men and women</u>, <u>at the office door</u>; 12. <u>in the red dress</u>, <u>down the street</u>; 13. <u>of morning</u>, <u>through the window</u>; 14. <u>we had yesterday</u>, <u>on streets</u>, <u>all over the city</u>; 15. <u>of red flowers</u>; 16. <u>of blackbirds</u>, <u>under that bridge</u>; 17. <u>from our school</u>; 18. <u>with brown eyes</u>, <u>across the room</u>, <u>with her left hand</u>; 19. <u>of our bus</u>, <u>to all his passengers</u>; 20. <u>at our house</u>, <u>on Saturday</u>; 21. <u>who speaks only English</u>, <u>with many customers</u>; 22. <u>who hit to left field</u>, <u>before the ball was thrown in</u>; 23. <u>that is well trained</u>, <u>well-trained</u>; 24. <u>in our parish</u>, <u>who comes to him</u>; 25. <u>who knows what she is doing</u>, <u>with great caution</u>

5. 1. Verb *wrote*, Subject *Lisa*, Direct object *letter*, Complement none, Indirect object *mother*, Modifiers *hastily, angry, her*
2. Verb *is*, Subject *Beethoven*, Direct object none, Complement *composer*, Indirect object none, Modifiers *greatest, of all time*
3. Verb *met*, Subject *I*, Direct object *friend*, Complement none, Indirect object none, Modifiers *While I was waiting for Jon, another, old*
4. Verb *is*, Subject *Michelle*, Direct object none, Complement *student*, Indirect object none, Modifiers *worst, in the junior class*
5. Verb *gave*, Subject *Democratic candidate*, Direct object *speech*, Complement none, Indirect object none, Modifiers *important, over the radio*
6. Verb *gave*, Subject *Nola*, Direct object *present*, Complement none, Indirect object *Marla*, Modifiers *very, expensive*
7. Verb *rose*, Subject *woman*, Direct object none, Complement none, Indirect object none, Modifiers *old, from her chair, near the window*
8. Verb *are*, Subject *critics*, Direct object none, Complement *authors*, Indirect object none, Modifiers *Literary, often, frustrated*
9. Verb *identified*, Subject *ornithologist*, Direct object *birds*, Complement none, Indirect object none, Modifiers *competent, many, rare*
10. Verb *has written*, Subject *Emma Dally*, Direct object *novels*, Complement none, Indirect object none, Modifiers *three, interesting, on modern English life*
11. Verb *gives*, Subject *Working*, Direct object *headaches*, Complement none, Indirect object *Gary*, Modifiers *far into the night, bad*
12. Verb *experience*, Subject *nations*, Direct object *difficulties*, Complement none, Indirect object none, Modifiers *Most, Third World, economic*
13. Verb *are*, Subject *automobiles*, Direct object none, Complement *burden*, Indirect object none, Modifiers *Old, to their users*
14. Verb *has been*, Subject *Life*, Direct object none, Complement *better*, Indirect object none, Modifiers *never, for this generation*
15. Verb *study*, Subject *I*, Direct object none, Complement none, Indirect object none, Modifiers *always, at night*
16. Verb *are*, Subject *puppies*, Direct object none, Complement *envy*, Indirect object none, Modifiers *new, of the neighbors*
17. Verb *was*, Subject *H. L. Mencken*, Direct object none, Complement *critic*, Indirect object none, Modifiers *irreverent*
18. Verb *made*, Subject *Kate*, Direct object *dresses*, Complement none, Indirect object *herself, friends*, Modifiers *attractive, her*
19. Verb *receive*, Subject *Actors*, Direct object *letters*, Complement none, Indirect object none, Modifiers *many, every day*
20. Verb *damages*, Subject *Poverty*, Direct object *lives*, Complement none, Indirect object none, Modifiers *of many rural children*
21. Verb *go*, Subject *We*, Direct object none, Complement none, Indirect object none, Modifiers *still, to the theater, as often as possible*
22. Verb *are*, Subject *prices*, Direct object none, Complement *high*, Indirect object none, Modifiers *Commodity, everywhere*

23. Verb *bleeds*, Subject *he*, Direct object none, Complement none, Indirect object none, Modifiers *When Dick cuts himself, for a long time*
24. Verb *fly*, Subject *airplanes*, Direct object none, Complement none, Indirect object none, Modifiers *Paper, rarely, for more than a few minutes*
25. Verb *is*, Subject *Fishing*, Direct object none, Complement *fun*, Indirect object none, Modifiers *great, once you have learned the fundamental skills*

6.
1. Some of us liked the program that night; many people were enthusiastic about it
2. Many voters misinterpreted the remarks of the candidate; she tried to restate her position
3. we considered the problem carefully
4. Willie lived a long and happy life; his time had come to die
5. They had many happy experiences
6. Cigarettes have long been known to be dangerous to health; many people continue to smoke
7. He wanted to join her in the new business; he had little capital to invest
8. its quality was poor
9. His first remarks were greeted with derision; the audience soon began to applaud
10. Well researched papers usually get higher marks than hastily prepared papers

7.
1. even though they passed Driver Education
2. none
3. after their children finished college
4. even though the rest of her family does
5. that she was not a friend of ours, he was
6. where she teaches remedial reading
7. she would surely meet the town's financial needs
8. since they save the traveler little time and contribute heavily to air pollution
9. none
10. who yawned steadily and audibly from the time the movie began

8. 1. across the winding river; 2. After her divorce; of her name; 3. pinned to the wall; 4. soon to be released by the towing airplane; 5. in hope, of snaring something, for dinner; 6. to be; 7. none; 8. of tea, in late afternoon, to survive, until evening; 9. In the library; 10. to pick up our gear and retreat to the nearest town as quickly as possible

Chapter 2

1. 1. Harpo Marx; comedian; 2. sky; parachutes; 3. cuisine; hamburgers; chicken wings; 4. Bill; coat; father; 5. Charity; home; 6. football; statue; Hamilton; 7. avenue; restoration; 8. speech; hour; 9. chairmen; order; 10. puppy; spots; nose; 11. hotel; casino; 12. neighbor; car; 13. world; Martin Luther King; 14. Love; world; 15. pens; handwriting; 16. train; Chicago; time; show; 17. Mary; roses; 18. fluid; stain; 19. woman; bus; danger; 20. Lois; seat; 21. Mary; sweater; father; 22. Joe; tire; car; 23. hands; 24. Bridge; cup; tea; 25. Planning; time

2.
1. *Librarians* (subject of verb), *people* (object of verbal), *books* (object of verbal)
2. *McDonald* (subject of verb), *farm* (direct object)
3. *zoo* (object of preposition), *Monday* (object of preposition), *year* (object of preposition)
4. *Piano* (modifier), *music* (subject of verb), *glass* (object of preposition), *wine* (object of preposition), *candlelight* (object of preposition)
5. *music* (direct object); *all* (direct object of verb) *said*
6. *child* (subject of verb), *front* (object of preposition), *car* (object of preposition), *chance* (direct object)
7. *Father* (subject of verb), *videos* (object of verbal)
8. *Louis* (subject of verb), *painter* (object of verbal), *illustrator* (object of verbal)

    9. *mountain* (object of preposition), *chairlift* (object of preposition)
  10. *Attending* (subject of verb), *church* (object of verbal), *Sundays* (object of preposition), *custom* (predicate complement), *family* (object of preposition)
  11. *wife* (subject of verb), *dishes* (object of verbal)
  12. *marrying* (subject of verb), *Avis* (object of verbal), *life* (direct object)
  13. *Sam* (indirect object), *ticket* (direct object), *football* (modifier), *game* (object of preposition)
  14. *Alfred* (indirect object), *sweater* (direct object), *father* (object of preposition)
  15. *family* (object of preposition), *laundry* (modifier), *day* (subject of verb), *event* (predicate complement)
  16. *Eyeglasses* (subject of verb), *sign* (predicate complement), *age* (object of preposition), *bifocals* (subject of verb)
  17. *Acura* (subject of verb), *car* (predicate complement), *investment* (direct object)
  18. *wine* (subject of verb), *California* (modifier), *grapes* (object of preposition)
  19. *Term* (modifier), *papers* (subject of verb), *research* (modifier), *papers* (direct object)
  20. *advantages* (object of verbal), *microwave* (modifier), *ovens* (object of preposition)
  21. *Sculpture* (subject of verb), *hobby* (predicate complement)
  22. *advice* (object of preposition), *doctor* (object of preposition), *Fred* (subject of verb), *cigarettes* (object of verbal), *day* (object of preposition)
  23. *cabbage* (subject of verb), *room* (direct object), *garden* (object of preposition)
  24. *Cindy* (subject of verb), *bourbon* (modifier), *whiskey* (direct object)
  25. *couch* (subject of verb), *room* (object of preposition)

3. 1. road (common), James (proper), wife (common), chains (common), family car (common)
    2. Siberia (proper), thousands (common), deer (common)
    3. Atlantic (proper), oil (common), New York (proper), Portugal (proper)
    4. students (common), college (common), cost (common), tuition (common)
    5. physics (common), textbooks (common), Lorimer (proper), students (common), exercises (common)
    6. seats (common), England (proper), tourists (common), play (common), night (common), week (common)
    7. people (common), restaurants (common), patronage (common)
    8. lexicographers (common), guardians (common), language (common)
    9. Bernard Malamud (proper), author (common), stories (common), books (common)
  10. Roger Casement (proper), patriot (common), traitor (common)

4. 1. foxes, 2. chiefs, 3. attorneys, 4. potatoes, 5. spoonfuls, 6. valleys, 7. formulas or formulae, 8. genera, genuses, 9. addenda, addendums, 10. knives, 11. laboratories, 12. vocabularies, 13. absences, 14. cupfuls, 15. babysitters, 16. crises, 17. diagnoses, 18. synopses, 19. athletics, 20. libraries, 21. Joneses, 22. quotas, 23. data, 24. booths, 25. buzzes, 26. axes, 27. loci, 28. skies, 29. echoes, 30. preferences, 31. loaves, 32. lives, 33. matrices, 34. actuaries, 35. bases, 36. neuroses, 37. privileges, 38. freshmen, 39. parentheses, 40. attorneys general, attorney generals, 41. analyses, 42. psychoses, 43. theses, 44. chassis, 45. quanta, 46. Smiths, 47. symphonies, 48. axes, 49. secretaries, 50. levities

5. 1. John's, 2. team's, 3. Nations', 4. Korea's, 5. Yankees', 6. Ruskin's, 7. neighbor's, 8. men's, 9. cook's, 10. Keats's, Keats', 11. wife's, 12. Year's, 13. Mickey's, 14. Johnsons', 15. Jones'

6. 1. singular, 2. singular, 3. plural, 4. plural, 5. singular, 6. singular, 7. plural, 8. singular, 9. singular, 10. plural

7. 1. Whether we go tomorrow or stay
    2. that we pool our remaining capital
    3. whatever came into his head first
    4. what happened during his job interview
    5. everything his children do

     6. what modern architecture can usually supply
     7. that the book was on reserve
     8. When the picnic is held
     9. Whatever you do
   10. Whoever attends the meeting

8.   1. a; 2. the; 3. the; 4. (none required); 5. a; 6. the; 7. An; 8. *an* honor to receive *the*; 9. *the* cabdrivers warned me not to stay at *the*; 10. An, The; 11. the, an; 12. *a* seaworthy sailboat, *the* ability to operate it, and *the*; 13. the; 14. (none required); 15. (none required)

Chapter 3

1.   1. verb *boarded*, subject *Richard*; verb *left*, subject *it*
     2. verb *found*, subject *defendant*
     3. verb *closed*, subject *door*; verb *left*, subject *she*
     4. verb *tolled*, subject *bell*; verb *gathered*, subject *people*
     5. verb *agreed*, subject *Eileen*; verb *was*, subject *trip*
     6. verb *remained*, subject *books*
     7. verb *was*, subject *Philosophy*; verb *earned*, subject *knowledge*
     8. verb *Eat*, subject *you* [understood]; verb *will have*, subject *you*
     9. verb *leaves*, subject *train*
   10. verb *played*, subject *children*; verb *were called*, subject *they*

2.   1. is no longer sharp enough to cut grass
     2. has not improved her outlook
     3. are hard to find in winter
     4. have not yet read the complete trial testimony
     5. has become big business all over the world
     6. Can ... imagine a world without war
     7. interrupted my sleep
     8. appears to be the main interest of America's young
     9. ran his tractor right into the haystack and ruined a week's work
   10. will one day reappear as a stylish fashion

3.   1. blackened transitive; 2. struck transitive, burned intransitive; 3. smiled intransitive; 4. hurts transitive; 5. indicated transitive; 6. gave transitive; 7. ran intransitive; 8. go intransitive; 9. incensed transitive; 10. attract transitive

4.   1. sounds copulative, correct predicate adjective; 2. seemed copulative, companions predicate noun; 3. became copulative, important predicate adjective; 4. act copulative, childish predicate adjective, are copulative, busy predicate adjective; 5. appeared copulative, uncanny predicate adjective; 6. was copulative, physician predicate noun; was copulative, available predicate adjective; 7. seemed copulative, eager predicate adjective; 8. grew copulative, lively predicate adjective; 9. acted copulative, sick predicate adjective; 10. was copulative, man predicate noun

5.   1. shall, 2. can, are, 3. is, 4. is, 5. is, 6. have, 7. Might, 8. Do, should, 9. are, 10. Would, 11. should, 12. have, 13. will, 14. is, 15. does

6.   1. should, 2. would, would, 3. should, 4. will, 5. should, 6. will, 7. will, 8. Would, 9. should, 10. would, 11. Will, 12. Shall, 13. will, 14. will, 15. should

7. 1. subjunctive,   2. subjunctive,   3. indicative,   4. indicative,   5. indicative,   6. imperative, 7. indicative,   8. indicative,   9. indicative,   10. subjunctive,   11. imperative,   12. indicative, 13. indicative,   14. indicative,   15. imperative

8. 1. forbid,   2. pay,   3. were,   4. insists,   5. were,   6. be,   7. Come,   8. be,   9. be,   10. were, 11. was,   12. be,   13. was,   14. were,   15. apologize

9. 1. passive,   2. active,   3. active,   4. active,   5. passive,   6. passive,   7. active,   8. passive,   9. active, 10. active

10. 1. will be going plural,   2. is singular,   3. is singular,   4. cooperate plural,   5. has been sitting singular, 6. Have been sitting plural,   7. will be leaving singular,   8. find plural,   9. will be having plural,   10. has seen singular

11. 1. have,   2. has,   3. is,   4. will achieve,   5. go,   6. collect,   7. are,   8. has,   9. finds,   10. are

12. 1. was,   2. are,   3. lie,   4. was,   5. is,   6. are,   7. is,   8. were,   9. are,   10. are

13. 1. is,   2. are,   3. wants,   4. carves,   5. are allowed,   6. are,   7. take,   8. goes,   9. are,   10. feeds, 11. swim,   12. is,   13. stand,   14. agree,   15. is,   16. has,   17. has,   18. were produced,   19. comfort, 20. carry

14. 1. expects,   2. votes,   3. makes,   4. are,   5. works,   6. leaves,   7. have,   8. amaze,   9. is,   10. is

15. 1. third person plural,   2. third person plural,   3. second person singular,   4. first person plural,   5. first person plural,   6. third person plural,   7. second person singular or plural,   8. first person singular, 9. third person plural,   10. third person plural

16. 1. present, active;   2. present perfect, passive;   3. present, active;   4. present perfect progressive, active;   5. future, active;   6. future progressive, active;   7. present, passive; present, passive;   8. present progressive, passive;   9. future, active;   10. past, passive;   11. past perfect, active;   12. present, passive; 13. past, active; past perfect, passive;   14. future, active;   15. present perfect, active

17. 1. diving,   2. ran,   3. fall,   4. wrung,   5. shown,   6. had led,   7. laid,   8. eaten,   9. got,   10. dove or dived,   11. lay,   12. shrank or shrunk,   13. lent,   14. rang or rung,   15. spoken

18. 1. will be,   2. have been eaten,   3. hurts,   4. became,   5. have raised,   6. will be,   7. calls,   8. Is, 9. inhale,   10. will leave,   11. had escaped,   12. will have left,   13. learned,   14. turns,   15. have

19. 1. liked,   2. had learned,   3. had been delivered,   4. gave,   5. like,   6. had missed,   7. watched, 8. waited,   9. comes,   10. will be or is,   11. was,   12. is,   13. had arrived,   14. are acted,   15. is

20. 1. was,   2. is,   3. entails,   4. will have,   5. will depart or departs,   6. use,   7. was,   8. was,   9. knew, portrayed,   10. will continue

21. 1. The first thing you should do is remove the wheel and then examine the brakes. *or* The first thing to do is remove the wheel and then examine the brakes.

2. Some writers work only four hours a day, because they cannot do creative work for longer periods.

3. They found that they could not sew the seams well, since they always made mistakes when they first tried to learn a new skill.

4. When one has little money to spend, one is careful about every purchase. *or* When you have little money to spend, you are careful about every purchase.

5. If you go to the dance, you will find unescorted women welcome.

6. Because he considered the design perfect, the judges ruled against him.

7. correct

8. He selected the material for the coat, and the tailor was then told to begin work.

9. The women had insisted on admitting men to their group, but most of the men found the meetings dull.

10. Nightmares disturb his sleep night after night, and he finds no relief in sedatives.

22. 1. complement, 2. adverb, 3. adverb, 4. noun, 5. adverb, 6. complement, 7. noun, 8. noun, 9. noun, 10. noun

23. 1. *the employees to complete the job on schedule*
Function of phrase: object of *ordered*; Functions of words: *the* modifies *employees*, *employees* is subject of infinitive *to complete*, *the* modifies *job*, *job* is object of *to complete*, prepositional phrase *on schedule* modifies *to complete*, *on* introduces prepositional phrase, *schedule* is object of preposition *on*

2. *To identify enemies*
Function of phrase: modifies *met*; Functions of words: *enemies* is object of infinitive *to identify*

3. *her to forget her achievements completely*
Function of phrase: object of *told*; Functions of words: *her* is subject of infinitive *to forget*, *her* modifies *achievements*, *achievements* is object of *to forget*, *completely* modifies *to forget*

4. *me to answer the phone in her absence*
Function of phrase: object of *asked*; Functions of words: *me* is subject of infinitive *to answer*, *the* modifies *phone*, *phone* is object of *to answer*, prepositional phrase *in her absence* modifies *to answer*, *in* introduces prepositional phrase, *her* modifies *absence*, *absence* is object of preposition *in*

5. *To achieve his ambition*
Function of phrase: subject of *required*; Functions of words: *his* modifies *ambition*, *ambition* is object of infinitive *to achieve*

24. 1. to have taken, 2. to forgive, 3. to delay, 4. to be fed, 5. to have been fed, 6. to tell, 7. to tell, 8. to play, 9. to admit, 10. to have prepared

25. 1. *to more than lose*; to lose more than
2. correct
3. *To more than two hours work overtime*; To work overtime more than two hours
4. *to not board the bus*; not to board the bus
5. *was to safe and sound find the child*; was to find the child safe and sound
6. *to firmly but respectfully demand*; to demand firmly but respectfully
7. *To have within a period of an hour walked around the park*; To have walked around the park within an hour
8. correct
9. *to without hesitation tell the entire story*; to tell the entire story without hesitation
10. *to without delay sell their car*; to sell their car without delay

26. 1. *Rushing* modifies *Christopher*, 2. *Having been told* modifies *Hillary*, 3. *Found* modifies *money*, 4. *Sustained* modifies *I*, 5. *locked* modifies *child*, 6. *Swallowing* modifies *boy*, 7. *Left* modifies *Felice*, 8. *Having refused* modifies *William*, 9. *Tired* modifies *attorney*, 10. *Congratulating* modifies *Hingis*

27. 1. Having been told, 2. Finding, 3. Having left, 4. Having refused, 5. Having offered, 6. arriving,
7. omitted, 8. challenging, 9. realizing, 10. having retired

28. 1. function: subject of verb; modifiers: none; object: none
2. function: object of verb; modifiers: *interesting* adjective; object: none
3. function: object of preposition; modifiers: none; object: none
4. function: object of verb; modifiers: none; object: none
5. function: complement of verb; modifiers: none; object: *enough*
6. function: subject of verb; modifiers: none; object: *specimens*
7. function: subject of verb; modifiers: *quickly to the bone* adverbial phrase; object: none
8. function: subject of verb; modifiers: *rapidly* adverb; object: *papers*
9. function: subject of verb; modifiers: *good* adjective; object: none
10. function: object of verb; modifiers: *his, tedious* adjectives; object: none

29. 1. For a company to sell that many automobiles, a great many people must like the design.
2. A plane will hit people standing in the runway.
3. The play having run for many weeks, most people considered it a success.
4. Before gaining admittance to his apartment, one must ring a bell.
5. After I had helped the old man cross the street, the rest of the walk was uneventful.
6. For the painting to achieve even modest acceptance, all aspects of it must be considered carefully.
7. correct
8. As I stumbled blindly in the fog, I saw a man appear.
9. Having assembled all the necessary ingredients, she is certain of a fine dinner.
10. To prepare a fine dinner, a cook must use fresh ingredients.

30. 1. correct, 2. are going to do badly, 3. correct, 4. correct, 5. are leaving by January, 6. correct,
7. are willing to take jobs, 8. to take an apartment, 9. correct, 10. and leaving their dying bodies

31. 1. and *can create* poor morale, 2. correct, 3. correct, 4. nor *lending* will lead, 5. but she *found*,
6. and *preserve* the independence, 7. correct, 8. and *ruining* the best, 9. correct, 10. both *boring
and* annoying, or: both a bore and *an annoyance*

Chapter 4

1. 1. pronoun *they*, pronoun *they*, antecedent *Kate and Leonard*; 2. pronoun *it*, antecedent *mouse*;
3. pronoun *he*, antecedent *painter*, pronoun *them*, antecedent *brushes*; 4. pronoun *he*, antecedent
Heinrich Böll; 5. pronoun *he*, pronoun *he*, antecedent *veteran*; 6. pronoun *he*, antecedent *John*,
pronoun *she*, antecedent *Sally*; 7. pronoun *they*, antecedent *John and Sally*, pronoun *she*, antecedent *Sally*;
pronoun *he*, antecedent *John*; 8. pronoun *it*, antecedent *game*, pronoun *they*, antecedent *words*;
9. pronoun *they*, pronoun *they*, antecedent *Joan and Audrey*; 10. pronoun *they*, antecedent *teachers and
parents*; 11. pronoun *it*, antecedent *tooth*; 12. pronoun *she*, antecedent *governor*, pronoun *it*, antecedent
proclamation; 13. pronoun *they*, antecedent *Zebras*; 14. pronoun *They*, antecedent *lessons*, pronoun *he*,
antecedent *Mr. Cunningham*; 15. pronoun *he*, pronoun *him*, antecedent *Dan*; 16. pronoun *they*,
antecedent *Textbooks*, pronoun *it*, antecedent *money*; 17. pronoun *she*, pronoun *she*, pronoun *she*,
antecedent *Mary*, pronoun *them*, antecedent *dishes*; 18. pronoun *her*, pronoun *she*, antecedent *Marjorie*;
19. pronoun *he*, antecedent *Jon*; 20. pronoun *she*, antecedent *Ruth*; 21. pronoun *they*, antecedent
advantages, pronoun *they*, antecedent *tourists*; 22. pronoun *they*, antecedent *bombs*; 23. pronoun *it*,
antecedent *Vermont*; 24. pronoun *all*, pronoun *them*, antecedent *citizens*; 25. pronoun *it*, antecedent
Chicago

2. 1. she, 2. he or she, 3. they, 4. She, 5. them, 6. They, it, 7. mine, 8. it, 9. They,
10. They, 11. he or she, 12. you, 13. their, 14. it, 15. her, 16. them, theirs, 17. them,
18. her, 19. she, 20. him, 21. They, 22. he or she, 23. it, 24. theirs, 25. hers

3. 1. which, 2. that, 3. who, 4. which, 5. whose, 6. that, 7. whom, 8. which, 9. that, 10. Whoever, 11. that, 12. Whomever or Whatever, 13. that, 14. Whichever, 15. which, 16. whomever, 17. that, 18. which, 19. whose, 20. that, 21. who, 22. whom, 23. Whoever, 24. Which or Whichever, 25. whom

4. 1. so, 2. these, those, 3. this or that, 4. those, 5. this or that or these or those, 6. first or last, 7. this, that, 8. these, those, 9. such, 10. Those

5. 1. Who, 2. What, 3. Which, 4. Whom, 5. What or Whom or Which, 6. Who, 7. What, 8. Who, 9. What, 10. What

6. 1. himself, 2. yourself, 3. themselves, 4. herself, 5. myself, oneself, 6. themselves, 7. herself 8. yourself, 9. himself, 10. herself, 11. yourselves, 12. myself, 13. herself, 14. herself, 15. itself

7. 1. ourselves, 2. itself, 3. himself, 4. oneself, 5. myself, 6. yourselves, 7. himself, 8. yourself or yourselves, 9. herself, 10. himself, 11. ourselves, 12. itself, 13. yourselves, 14. yourself or yourselves, 15. yourself or yourselves

8. 1. one another's, 2. one another, 3. each other, 4. each other's, 5. one another or each other, 6. one another's or each other's, 7. one another's, 8. one another, 9. each other, 10. one another

9. 1. everyone, 2. No one or Nobody, 3. no one or nobody, 4. anything, 5. All or Many or Several, 6. anyone or anybody or everybody or everyone, 7. everything or more or all, 8. little or nothing, 9. little or nothing or everything or something, 10. nothing or little, 11. Anyone or Everyone or Anybody or Everybody, 12. anything, 13. Much or Everything; little or nothing, 14. all or everything; everybody or everyone, 15. No one or Nobody, 16. everyone or everybody; no one or nobody, 17. such, 18. few, 19. someone or somebody, 20. Everyone or Everybody, 21. everyone or everybody, 22. Many, few, 23. no one or nobody, 24. someone or somebody, 25. others

10. 1. it, 2. they, 3. they, 4. they, 5. who, themselves, 6. Which, 7. it, 8. they, 9. one, 10. he, they, 11. it, they, 12. they, they, 13. who, himself, 14. who, who, he, 15. those, she, 16. it, 17. he, 18. it, 19. Which, 20. which, itself, 21. they, he, 22. they, it, 23. she, it, 24. he, it, 25. he, who, him

11. 1. it, 2. they, 3. they, 4. hers, 5. her, 6. them, 7. them, 8. they, 9. them, 10. they

12. 1. it, 2. they, 3. it, 4. it, 5. they, 6. they, 7. it, 8. themselves, 9. it, 10. it

13. 1. who, 2. he or she, himself or herself, 3. he or she, 4. itself, 5. himself or herself, himself or herself 6. it, 7. it, 8. herself, 9. his or hers, 10. herself, 11. it, 12. herself, 13. it, 14. himself or herself, 15. himself, 16. it, 17. he or she, 18. it, 19. he or she, 20. he or she

14. 1. It or This or That, 2. Who, 3. she, 4. he, 5. he, 6. they, 7. they, 8. I, 9. who, 10. who, he or she, he or she

15. 1. her, her, 2. whom, 3. Whom, 4. me, 5. us, 6. them, 7. me, you, 8. him, 9. Whom, 10. her

16. 1. them, 2. them, 3. them, 4. it, 5. them, 6. him, 7. it, 8. them, 9. them, 10. her or him

17. 1. her or him or it, 2. them or you or us, 3. me or you or us or him or her, 4. him, 5. him or her, 6. her, 7. whom, 8. him, 9. them or you or us, them, 10. her

18. 1. his or hers or yours or theirs, 2. theirs, 3. Whose, 4. ours, 5. hers, 6. ours, 7. ours, 8. mine or yours or his or hers, 9. mine, 10. ours

19. 1. me, 2. I, 3. mine, 4. him, 5. I, 6. me, 7. mine, 8. mine or ours, 9. me, 10, I

Chapter 5

1. 1. Ten, enough, two, large, 2. Oaken, early, 3. only, little, 4. Hard, great, 5. orange, advisable, ski

2. 1. *Improper* descriptive, *her* limiting, *catering* descriptive
2. *Careful* descriptive, *several* limiting, *his* limiting, *experimental* descriptive
3. *Mexican* proper; *his* limiting
4. *Poor* descriptive, *his* limiting, *Irish* proper
5. *One* limiting, *perfect* descriptive

3. 1. *His* possessive, *his* possessive, 2. *Eleven* numerical, 3. *her* possessive, *her* possessive, 4. *That* demonstrative, *both* indefinite, *my* possessive, 5. *What* interrogative, 6. *whose* relative, *all* indefinite, 7. *Each* indefinite, *his* possessive, 8. *No* indefinite, 9. *whose* relative, 10. *Their* possessive, 11. *His* possessive, 12. *Which* interrogative, *her* possessive, 13. *first* numerical, *her* possessive, 14. *That* demonstrative, *only* indefinite, *your* possessive, 15. *Any* indefinite

4. 1. fine, 2. excellent, 3. exciting, 4. bad, 5. better, 6. radiant, 7. larger, 8. (none), 9. disconsolate, 10. sad

5. 1. fresh trout, 2. Rare books, 3. Italian opera, 4. ripe pear, 5. so exciting

6. 1. better, 2. smaller, 3. youngest, 4. more suitable or less suitable, 5. broadest, 6. more competent or less competent, 7. best, 8. best, 9. longer, 10. longest

7. 1. between you and me, 2. for indigent persons, 3. with failing businesses, 4. with little hope, 5. with substantial fortunes, about the stock market, 6. between houses, in my town, 7. of the Impressionist paintings, in the United States, 8. through my window, 9. to Europe, 10. on his right lung

8. 1. that had been missing for many years, 2. which are indigenous to Africa, 3. who are skillful in interpreting scientific data, 4. who find their immediate desires blocked, 5. that have been stored properly, 6. I have treasured since childhood, 7. that had managed to survive without care, 8. he plans to cook today, 9. she felled with her little hatchet, 10. who has ever found himself unable to find a job, who are habitually unemployed

9.   1. he wrote in his English courses (restrictive)
2. that were active in the period between the two world wars (restrictive)
3. that have been left unrefrigerated (restrictive)
4. that have served their masters well (restrictive)
5. that conveys gratitude but little warmth (restrictive)
6. I consult most often (restrictive)
7. , who have made many important cultural contributions to our country, (nonrestrictive)
8. , which has a distinctive texture and appearance, (nonrestrictive)
9. , which calls itself the world leader in maple syrup production (nonrestrictive)
10. , which is a relatively new phenomenon, (nonrestrictive)

10.   1. The pipe that I left behind was one of the best I ever owned.
2. My last dollar, which I wanted to spend on food, was supposed to keep me alive until payday.
3. Two quarts of milk, which cost less than a pound of meat, have more food value as far as I am concerned.
4. Yesterday's newspaper, which was left on my doorstep, belongs to my neighbor.
5. The message that the fiery minister conveys is not to be ignored.

11.   1. book, 2. Farmer, 3. police, store, 4. Phonograph, music, 5. furniture

12.   1. proud, 2. poor, 3. swift, 4. wealthy, indigent, 5. learned

13.   1. sold, 2. Undeterred, 3. Struggling, 4. Sprinkled, 5. victimized, 6. unopened, 7. finding, unrewarding, 8. Harassed, dispirited, 9. Gasping, 10. achieved

14.   1. Running as hard as possible, I could not catch my breath.
2. correct
3. After having walked in circles for three hours, I knew I had lost my way.
4. Since many people at that college were studious, the library was heavily used.
5. Once it is cooked, I can enjoy a fine roast.
6. correct
7. correct
8. A feeling of despair is no surprise in one stuck in traffic for hours.
9. While sitting quietly before a wood fire, young and old find noisy children a nuisance.
10. Upon meeting old friends, one naturally responds with pleasure.

15.   1. to acquit—*vote*, 2. to suit the happy occasion—*food*, 3. to feed them—*owners*, 4. to dance to—*music*, 5. to read—*biography*, 6. to meet every situation—*joke*, 7. to use for this job—*tool*, 8. to miss Sunday services—*permission*, 9. to wear—*clothes*, 10. to cover the story—*reporter*

Chapter 6

1.   1. *quietly* modifies *weep*; 2. *completely* modifies *honest*; 3. *Ideally* modifies *the doctor will have completed her examination*; 4. *partially* modifies *closed*, *usually* modifies *ineffective*, *quietly* modifies *spoken*; 5. *diligently* modifies *practice*, *never* modifies *satisfy*; 6. *patiently* modifies *sat*, *finally* modifies *withdrew*; 7. *quite* modifies *carefully*, *carefully* modifies *works*; 8. *Subsequently* modifies *we discussed the bill with the manager*; 9. *openly* modifies *rebuked*, *fairly* modifies *obvious*; 10. *never* modifies *can work*, *too* modifies *carefully*, *carefully* modifies *can work*

2.   1. adjective, 2. adverb, 3. adverb, 4. adverb, 5. adverb, 6. adjective, 7. adverb, 8. adverb, 9. adjective, 10. adverb, 11. adverb, 12. adjective, 13. adverb, 14. adverb, 15. adverb

3. 1. sometimes, time, 2. possibly, manner, 3. almost, manner, 4. awkwardly, manner, 5. never, time, 6. frugally, manner, 7. Finally, time, 8. ever, time; there, place, 9. less, degree, 10. soon, time, 11. Yes, assertion, 12. undoubtedly, assertion, 13. guardedly, manner, 14. quickly, manner, 15. west, place

4. 1. adverb, 2. adverb, 3. adverb, 4. adjective, 5. adverb, 6. adjective, 7. adverb, 8. adjective, 9. adjective, 10. adverb, 11. adjective, 12. adverb, 13. adjective, 14. adjective, 15. adverb

5. 1. more comfortably, 2. more deeply, 3. more or less lovingly, 4. more vividly, 5. most colorfully, 6. longer, 7. more hungrily, 8. most hotly, 9. most heavily, 10. most heavily

6. 1. beyond the last house; on their street, 2. mornings, 3. in the morning, 4. In the cool evenings; after dinner, 5. in the Flemish manner, 6. at the box office, 7. Sundays; on television, 8. ten minutes, 9. five hundred thousand dollars, 10. twenty pounds more than her younger sister

7.
1. *that I could no longer remain in the room* (result), modifies main clause
2. *Had I paid adequate attention in class* (condition), modifies main clause
3. *as if he did not care at all about my feelings* (manner), modifies verb *behaved*
4. *than most of his contemporaries* (comparison), modifies *profound*
5. *provided that she signed the dormitory register upon leaving* (condition), modifies main clause
6. *wherever you drive in New Jersey* (place), modifies main clause
7. *because I had reached the age of eighteen* (cause), modifies main clause
8. *even though the plagiarism committee questioned him all day* (condition), modifies verb *would submit*
9. *Before you gather up your books* (time), modifies main clause
10. *Since a quorum is not present* (cause), modifies main clause
11. *Although he tried every trick he knew* (concession), modifies main clause
12. *If no one shows up for the picnic* (condition), modifies main clause
13. *as I was crossing the street* (time), modifies main clause
14. *as I had in my first term* (comparison), modifies adjective *good*
15. *Had I remembered what the instructor told me* (condition), modifies main clause
16. *as their masters have taught them* (manner), modifies verb *do behave*
17. *Because there was nothing left to do but surrender* (cause), modifies main clause
18. *whenever I can find a replacement* (time), modifies infinitive *to leave*
19. *if colleges maintain academic standards* (condition), modifies main clause
20. *since it was painted* (time), modifies main clause
21. *as if she was thoroughly exhausted* (manner), modifies main clause
22. *Since there are only four of us* (cause), modifies main clause
23. *Although nothing appeared to be wrong with the car* (concession), modifies main clause
24. *Wherever I go in New York* (place), modifies main clause
25. *While I was having my lunch* (time), modifies verb *dropped by*

8.
1. I insist on going to the baseball game; I insist, moreover, that you go with me.
2. The organization treasury is completely empty; it will, nevertheless, continue to attempt to raise funds so that it can pay its debts.
3. The final date for submittal of proposals has not yet passed; we will, therefore, receive all properly executed offers until that date arrives.
4. Complete agreement between the two contestants is not likely; however, we can always hope that both parties will somehow see that their interests lie in mutual trust.
5. The patient shows no signs of recovering despite all the medical treatment he has been given; thus, there is nothing to do but hope that careful nursing and the processes of nature will see him through.

9. 1. *extremely* (keep), 2. *much* (keep), 3. *too* (keep), 4. *somewhat* (delete), 5. *tremendously* (delete), 6. *extremely* (delete), 7. *quite* (delete), 8. *very* (delete), 9. *quite* (delete), 10. *too* (keep)

10. 1. *to become violent* modifies *tends*, 2. *to cover several Southern states* modifies *seems*, 3. *to repeal the abortion laws* modifies *were introduced*, 4. *to utilize his great speed* modifies *bats*, 5. *[to] mock anyone* modifies *didn't dare*, 6. *to travel to Scotland again this summer* modifies *intend*, 7. *to drink a great deal of water* modifies *are inclined*, 8. *to evict his objectionable tenant* modifies *tried*, 9. *to stock their shelves with worthwhile books* modifies *eager*, 10. *to travel on their own* modifies *love*

Chapter 7

1. 1. for hepatitis, by the doctor; 2. from Little Rock; 3. to the theater, with her father; 4. at the seashore, during the entire summer; 5. in time, for the late flight; 6. On two occasions, with the dentist; 7. For all; 8. with color, in the autumn; 9. in the house, for lunch; 10. for charitable purposes

2. 1. (of) economic recession, 2. (for) work, 3. (of) my friends, (at) the reunion, 4. (for) which I have been waiting, 5. (to) stadium, (in) dread, (of) afternoon, 6. (by) Beethoven, 7. (from) nursery, (to) room, 8. (of) arrival, (of) spring, (of) how cold spring can be, 9. (of) studies, (of) sciences, 10. (for) Antarctica, (in) months

3. 1. *During the raid* modifies *were wounded* (verb)
   2. *in the bus station* modifies *lost* (verb)
   3. *by the reviewing stand* modifies *passed* (verb)
   4. *By the end* modifies *was left* (verb), *of the performance* modifies *end* (noun), *in the audience* modifies *was left* (verb)
   5. *to our school* modifies *close* (adjective)
   6. *for his courtesy* modifies *was rewarded* (verb), *by the old woman* modifies *was rewarded* (verb)
   7. *in his coin collection* modifies *delight* (noun)
   8. *to the hospital* modifies *way* (noun)
   9. *by some people* modifies *is recognized* (verb)
   10. *with great care* modifies *selected* (verb)

4. 1. Throughout the term, 2. into a major exercise, 3. past the guardrail, onto the lawn, 4. for their inexpensive white and red wines, 5. Across town, like that, of France, 6. within reason, 7. Because of his delay, in paying, 8. Out of the pitch black night, of threatening appearance, 9. near the city center, in city life, 10. past the maître d'hôtel, near the band, 11. off the stage, of her legs, 12. Since her husband's death, of her own, 13. instead of you, 14. In spite of everything, 15. toward the bar, despite my repeated warnings

5. 1. her, 2. you, 3. us, 4. whomever, 5. her, them, 6. them, 7. him, 8. her, 9. Whom, 10. me, her

6. 1. none, 2. for, 3. but, 4. for, because of, 5. for, with, 6. none, 7. of, 8. none, 9. after, but, 10. For

7. 1. adverb, adverb, 2. adjective, adverb, 3. adverb, adverb, 4. adjective, adjective, 5. adjective, adverb, adjective, 6. adjective, adverb, 7. adjective, adjective, 8, adverb, 9. adjective, adverb, 10. adjective, adjective

8. 1. Of all the members, of doing such mischief, 2. on a little hill, behind the wall, for someone, 3. in offices, with copying machines, 4. with good tobacco, 5. Near the farm, to the making, of lime, 6. none, 7. by the firehouse, during her lunch hour, 8. In the afternoons, about the city, for some diversion, in his misery,   9.   with smoke, on the upper floors,   10.   none,   11.   in full leaf,   12.   of my time, on chores, of completion,   13.   in tormenting children,   14.   For days, on end, to the sidewalk,   15.   In the afternoons, for her eyes, to the subdued light, of the nursing home

9.   1.   *Not only ... but* coordinating;   2.   *so that* subordinating;   3.   *Since* subordinating, *and* coordinating;   4.   *Until* subordinating, *and* coordinating;   5.   *Either ... or* coordinating, *because* subordinating;   6.   *When* subordinating, *so* subordinating;   7.   *or* coordinating, *yet* coordinating;   8.   *or* coordinating, *when* subordinating;   9.   *So* subordinating, *that* subordinating, *and* coordinating;   10.   *Wherever* subordinating, *or* coordinating, *that* subordinating

INDEX

Printed in the USA
CPSIA information can be obtained
at www.ICGtesting.com
LVHW072013300124
770226LV00007B/910